Spiritual
e–Soup™

Future Books by Author

Spiritual Humor e-Soup: A Compilation of Amusing Messages from the Internet

Humorous e-Soup: A Compilation of Jokes from the Internet

Spiritual e-Soup™

A Compilation of Inspirational Messages from the Internet

RALPH BARNETT

For information contact:
e-Soup Publishing
994 Glenwood Station Lane
Charlottesville, Virginia 22901-5709

(847) 606-0854
www.e-soupministry.com
info@e-soupministry.com

Library of Congress Cataloging-in-Publication data:
Barnett, Ralph.
Spiritual e-soup: a compilation of inspirational
messages from the Internet. Volume one / Ralph Barnett.
-- 1st ed.
p. cm.
ISBN-13: 978-0-9790903-0-1
ISBN-10: 0-9790903-0-X

1. Spiritual life. I. Title.

BL624.B376 2007 204'.4
QBI06-600543

2006910405
10 9 8 7 6 5 4 3 2 1
Printed on acid-free paper in the United States

Dedication/Acknowledgments

The one and only true God of Abraham who is my inspiration

Margaret, my wife, who is my Archangel

Marta, my daughter, who is my Angel

Brian, my son-in-law, the author of the "e-Soup" name

Anne Louque, my indispensable book producer and illustrator

The "Circle of e-Mail Friends" who contributed stories

The Keswick Club in Charlottesville, Va., my main office

Starbucks in Charlottesville, Va., my backup offices

Contents

Introduction

Electronic mail, e-mail, attracted my attention in the late 1990s. My sales training job kept me occupied in the classroom by day and exhausted at night due to the demands of travel. My window of opportunity for traditional communications was very narrow. After discovering the efficacy of e-mailing at any time, day or night, I quickly became an advocate.

At first, my e-mailing consisted of business topics but soon other types of e-mails appeared: jokes, inspirational, political, cultural, and personal. I eagerly collected e-mail addresses from family and friends for my newly adopted means of reaching out and touching someone.

Evolving into a rabid e-mailer, I sent, received, replied, and forwarded e-mails as fast as my ISP could disseminate them. So enthralled with the ability to e-mail widely and rapidly, discriminating between the variety of content did not enter my mind. If someone sent it to me, I forwarded it.

I was having the time of my life until a small, still, but elusive, voice muttered, "Ralph, maybe you should not forward vulgar jokes." I stopped forwarding crude jokes.

Later, the small, still, but vague, voice murmured, "Ralph, maybe you should not forward political proclamations." I stopped forwarding political statements.

Again, the small, still, but clearer, voice whispered, "Ralph, maybe you should not forward any jokes." I stopped forwarding jokes of any sort.

Finally, the small, still, but unmistakable, voice commanded, "Ralph, forward e-mails carrying the Good Word only." I recalled Matthew 28:19 where Jesus conferred the Great Commission upon the apostles. The Lord had instructed me to establish an electronic evangelical ministry to spread the Word to the ends of the earth.

My spiritual e-mail ministry was inaugurated in 2003. Continuing to receive e-mails of every stripe, I forwarded spiritual messages. Subscription to the ministry was, of course, free and voluntary. As a result, I received more and more spiritual missives which, after forwarding, were archived.

From time to time, I slipped in a joke that passed strict spiritual scrutiny in hopes that the Lord would overlook my stretching of authority. Shortly after, the small, still, but amused, voice of the Lord admitted, "You're right, Ralph, the spiritual jokes are too clever to deny. Include them in your ministry." I followed His order with a smile in my heart.

Response to the ministry surprised me. Members frequently remarked about how they enjoyed the messages and forwarded them to their contact lists. Friends and family of members e-mailed their appreciation of my ministry. It was not uncommon to receive replies such as "I truly needed that encouragement today," "This e-mail hit the spot," "My friend e-mailed me about how powerful this e-mail was for them," and others. My seed germinated and a vine with multiple branches soon formed.

Early on, I censored e-mails I concluded were unworthy or duplicates only to be chastised by the small, still voice. "Ralph, you are a conduit. E-mails do not come to you by mistake. Your duty is to forward them for as wide a distribution as possible. Let the Holy Spirit worry about their impact." In His mysterious way, e-mails previously censored by me received rave reviews by recipients.

The upbeat response to the e-mail ministry encouraged me to embark on producing a book composed of inspirational e-mails: e-Soup Ministry Publishing was born. My archives contained more than one thousand spiritual e-mails and jokes. The challenge was to edit, select the "best of," and sequence them for inclusion in the book.

None of these tasks was easy. Reading the messages in e-mail format divulges the theme but does not reveal edits and revisions required to meet publishing standards. Copy-editing proved time-consuming and tedious but exhilarating—consider the uplifting content.

Selection proved the most complex: how do you measure the relative worth of these invaluable masterpieces? First, I extracted the jokes for a separate book, *Spiritual Humor e-Soup* to be available in early 2007. This edition of *Spiritual e-Soup* contains 181 messages; 181 out of 500! God, help me. I am considering publishing a second volume. Your response to volume I will tell me whether to produce volume II.

After the arduous selection process, I eagerly approached sequencing with a preconceived notion: "No problem, Ralph, sort them into chapters by topic such as friends, Christmas, and so on." "So on" turned into a huge miscellaneous file containing many of the finest subjects.

At wits' end, it struck me that e-mails arrived in my inbox randomly, i.e., in His mysterious plan; perhaps the order of the book should be at random. My thought, *Hey, I'm doing His work; He'll take care of it.* You be the judge of the sequencing.

Lastly, actually "firstly," I welcome you to *Spiritual e-Soup* with the following message:

I have this circle of e-mail friends,
Who mean the world to me;
Some days I send and send,
At other times, I let them be.

I am so blessed to have these friends,
With whom I've grown so close;
So this little poem I dedicate to them,
For to me they are the most.

When I see each name download,
And view the e-mail they've sent;
I know they've thought of me that day,
And "well wishes" were their intent.

So to you, my friends, I'd like to say
Thank you for being a part
Of all my daily contacts,
This comes right from my heart.

God bless you is my prayer today,
I'm honored to call you friend;
I pray the Lord will keep you safe,
Until we e-mail again.

—Ralph Barnett

Note: Wherever the word "Christmas" appears in this book, you will see it spelled "CHRISTmas."

✝ The Lord Works in Mysterious Ways and in His Own Time ✝

June 30, 1981, was one of the most glorious days of my life—and I didn't even know it. Caught in a loveless, childless marriage, I was a workaholic who believed everything was in my hands. As a card-carrying member of the secular, post-Christian America, I thought I was in control.

But on this date, on the other side of the world in Warsaw, Poland, my daughter was born to a young, Polish couple. They named her Marta Maria. Marta was born at the time when Poland's union, Solidarity, was in revolution against the Communist government.

Her mother used her ration coupons to buy scarce, bare essentials for Marta. Her grandfather received aid from his church, aid that came from America. Her mother made a promise that if she ever came to America she would like to, personally, "find and thank the nice American family named Campbell that sent soup for us to eat."

I was living a life of luxury while my daughter was struggling for basics. On an endless treadmill of workaholism, I tried to drown the frustration of the emotional void in my marriage and my life. I was feeling sorry for myself while my daughter did not even have a dad; he had left—and I didn't even know it.

A small voice deep inside admonished me, "You need to change your ways." The Lord was working on me in his mysterious ways. Unknowingly following His advice, I moved to Hilton Head, S.C., to change my lifestyle, still believing I was in control.

My daughter was growing up in Poland under the loving care of her mother, Margaret, and her grandparents, Alina and Mieczyslaw. The Lord must have been speaking to Margaret in His mysterious way because she was having Marta tutored in English. But Marta, growing up without a dad, was developing an emotional void in her heart—and I didn't even know it.

After a few years on Hilton Head, my wife and I separated and I began to hear that small voice inside a little clearer. I attended church for the first time in thirty years, prayed to God, and discerned the small voice with more clarity.

Speaking to the Lord, I asked His forgiveness. He answered, "Not to worry, Ralph, your earthly thirty years are but a second to me." I fervently prayed, "Please, dear Lord, send me someone I can love. I have a void in my heart and a lot of love to give." But He did not answer.

About the same time, Marta's mother, Margaret, listening to a small voice inside, decided on a huge risk to fly to America searching for work as an architect.

The Lord, working in his mysterious way, directed her to an opportunity on Hilton Head. Marta, my daughter, was eleven and a half years old and in America.

I met Margaret and Marta in November, 1992, and Margaret and I married in March, 1993. In my earthly wisdom, I praised the Lord for answering my prayer by sending Margaret for me to give all my love. Wrong again—and I didn't even know it.

February 12, 1999 was one of the most glorious days of my life—and I did know it. For two weeks, I had been praying to God for help with a love letter to Marta. He finally answered, "Ralph, I sent Margaret to be your loving wife, the angel to take care of you. But I sent Marta to be your daughter so that you could fill the deep void left by her biological father.

"I sent Marta to fill the void left in your heart by a childless first marriage. Marta's the angel I sent for you to take care of with your love: She's the answer to your prayer of seven years ago. That is why you are walking her down the aisle at her Homecoming."

I cried to the Lord, "What took you so long to tell me?"

He responded, "Ralph, you know I work in my own time. And besides, she is already a beautiful seventeen-year-old and you will be walking her down another aisle soon to give her away."

I replied evenly, "Okay, Lord, give me one of *your* seconds to think about that."

✝ Will God Know Your Voice? ✝

The rancher went out to repair a distant fence.
The wind was cold and gusty, the clouds gray and dense.
As he pounded the last staples in and gathered tools to go,
The temperature had fallen; and the snow began to blow.

When he started up his pickup, he felt a heavy heart.
From the sound of the ignition, he knew it wouldn't start.
So Jake did what most of us would do if we'd been there.
He humbly bowed his balding head and sent aloft a prayer.

As he turned the key for the last time, he softly cursed his luck.
They found him three days later, frozen stiff in that old truck.

Now Jake had been around in life and done his share of roaming.
But arriving in Heaven shocked him. It looked just like Wyoming.

Of all the saints in Heaven, his favorite was St. Peter.
Now, this line ain't needed but it helps with rhyme and meter.
So they set and talked a minute, or maybe it was three.
Nobody was keepin' score—in Heaven time is free.

"I've always heard," Jake said to Pete, "That God'll answer prayer,
But one time I asked for help, well, He just plain wasn't there.
Does God answer prayers of some, and ignore the prayers of others?
That don't seem exactly square, I know all men are brothers.

"Or does He randomly reply, without good rhyme or reason?
Maybe, it's the time of day, the weather, or the season.
Now I ain't trying to act smart, it's just the way I feel.
And I was wondering, could you tell me what is the deal?"

St. Peter listened very patiently and when Jake was done,
With smiles of recognition, he said, "So, you are the one.
That day your truck wouldn't start, and you sent a prayer a' flying,
You gave us all a real bad time, with bunches of us trying.

A hundred angels rushed to check the status of your file,
But ya' know, Jake, we hadn't heard from you in quite a while.
And though all prayers are answered, 'cause God ain't got no quota,
He didn't know your voice and started a truck in Minnesota."

✝ Checking in Today ✝

A minister passing through his church in the middle of the day
Decided to pause by the altar and see who had come to pray.
Suddenly the back door opened, a man came down the aisle,
The minister frowned for he saw the man hadn't shaved in a while.
His shirt was kinda' shabby and his coat was worn and frayed,
The man knelt, bowed his head, then rose and walked away.

In the days that followed, noontime saw this chap,
Each time he knelt for a moment, a lunch pail in his lap.
Well, the minister's suspicions grew, with robbery a main fear,
He decided to stop the man and ask, "What are you doing here?"
The man said, "I work down the road and lunch is half an hour.
Lunchtime is my prayer time, for finding strength and power.

"I stay only moments, you see, the factory's so far away;
As I kneel here talking to the Lord, this is kinda' what I say:
'I just came again to tell you, Lord, how happy I have been
Since we found each other's friendship and you took away my sin.
Don't know much of how to pray, but I think about you every day.
So, Jesus, this is Jim checking in again today.'"

The minister, feeling foolish, told Jim, "That's fine.
You're welcome to come and pray anytime."
"Time to go," Jim smiled and said as he hurried to the door.
The minister knelt at the altar; he'd never done it before.
His cold heart melted, warmed with love, he met with Jesus there.
As the tears flowed, in his heart, he repeated ole Jim's prayer:
"I just came again to tell you, Lord, how happy I've been
Since we found each other's friendship and you took away my sin.
I don't know much of how to pray, but I think about you every day.
So, Jesus, this is me checking in again today."

Past noon one day, the minister noticed that Jim hadn't come.
As more days passed without him, he began to worry some.
He went to the factory, and learned that Jim was ill.
The hospital staff was worried, but he'd given them a thrill.
The week that Jim was with them brought changes in the ward;
His smiles, a joy contagious. Changed people were his reward.
The head nurse couldn't understand why Jim was so glad,
When no flowers, calls, or cards came, not a visitor he had.

The minister stayed by his bed, he voiced the nurse's concern:
No friends came to show they cared. He had nowhere to turn.
Looking surprised, old Jim spoke up, and with a winsome smile:
"The nurse is wrong, she couldn't know, that in here all the while
Each day at noon He's here, a dear friend of mine, you see,
He sits right down, takes my hand, leans over, and says to me,
'I just came again to tell you, Jim, how happy I have been,
Since we found this friendship, and I took away your sin.
Always love to hear you pray, I think about you every day,
And so, Jim, this is Jesus checking in again today.'"

✝ I Never Found the Time ✝

I knelt to pray but not for long,
I had too much to do.
I had to hurry and get to work
For bills would soon be due.

So I knelt and said a hurried prayer,
And jumped up off my knees.
My Christian duty was now done
My soul could rest at ease.

All day long I had no time
To spread a word of cheer.
No time to speak of Christ to friends,
They'd laugh at me I'd fear.

No time, no time, too much to do,
That was my constant cry,
No time to give to souls in need
But came at last, the time to die.

I went before the Lord,
I came, I stood with downcast eyes.
For in his hands God held a book,
It was the Book of Life.

God looked into His book and said,
"Your name I cannot find.
I once was going to write it down
But never found the time."

⌖ The Difference between Rich and Poor People ⌖

The father of a wealthy family took his son to the countryside for the purpose of showing him how the poor live. They spent a week on a farm of a poor family. On their return, the father asked, "My son, how was the trip?"

"It was great, Dad."

"Did you see how poor people live?" the father inquired.

"Oh yeah," responded the son.

"Tell me what you learned," requested the father.

The son answered, "I learned:

We have one dog; they have four.

We have a pool reaching to the middle of our garden; they have a creek that has no end.

We have imported lanterns in our garden; they have the stars.

Our patio extends to the front yard; they have a whole horizon.

We have a small piece of land to live on; they have fields that go beyond sight.

We have servants who serve us; they serve others.

We buy our food; they grow theirs.

We have walls around our property to protect us; they have friends to protect them."

The boy's father was speechless.

His son added, "Thanks, Dad, for showing me how poor we are."

When you change the way you look at things,
things begin to change the way they look.

✥ Your Loving Friend ✥

As you awoke, I hoped you would talk to me, even if only a few words, asking my opinion or thanking me for some good in your life. But I noticed you were busy trying to find the right outfit to wear.

When you rushed to get ready, I knew there would be a moment for you to pause and say, "Hello," but you were too busy. At one point, you sat in a chair for fifteen minutes with nothing to do. When you sprang to your feet, I thought you wanted to talk to me but you ran to the phone and called a friend for the latest gossip instead.

I patiently watched all day. With your activities, I guess you were too busy to speak to me. At lunch, you looked around and I thought maybe you did not bow your head because you felt embarrassed to talk to me. You noticed some friends talking to me before they ate, but you did not. That is okay; there is time left and I hope you will talk to me yet.

You went home and had chores to do. Afterward, you turned on the TV where about anything goes. You spend lots of time in front of it not thinking at all. I waited again as you ate your meal but you declined to talk to me.

At bedtime, I guess you felt too tired. After saying goodnight to your family, you plopped into bed and fell fast asleep. That is okay; you may not realize I am always there for you. I have patience; more than you will ever know. I want to teach you to be patient with others as well.

I love you so much that I wait each day for a prayer, a thought, or a thankful part of your heart. It is hard to have a one-sided dialogue.

You are getting up and, again, I will wait with nothing but love for you. Hoping that today you will give me some time. Have a nice day.

Your loving friend, God

✥ Power of Prayer ✥

If Christians truly comprehended the extent of the power available through prayer, we would be speechless.

In World War II, an advisor to Winston Churchill organized a group who dropped what they were doing every day at a prescribed hour for one minute to collectively pray for the safety of England, its troops, its people, and peace.

A dedicated prayer activity is being organized in the United States. If you would like to participate—each evening at 8:00 CST, stop what you are doing for one minute and pray for the safety of our country, our troops, our citizens, and peace. Prayer is our most powerful asset and together we can make a difference.

O Father, Who art in heaven, thou Who has given us birth,
Lend us thy flaming sword, O Lord, to fight thy battle on earth.
As we walk through the perilous darkness, lend us thy holy light
That shines in thy heavenly mansion to guide our path at night.
And lend thy shield and armor to the gallant boys over there.
They are thy children, Father, and this is thy country's prayer:
That soon may the forces of evil fall at last on their knees,
With the flag of thy kingdom of heaven flying high in the breeze.
Sons will return to their mothers and men to their wives from this fight
And, this earth will be like heaven, both peaceful and bright.

✟ Train of Life ✟

Some folks ride the train of life looking out the rear,
Watching miles of life roll by and marking every year.
They sit in sad remembrance of wasted days gone by,
And curse their life for what it was, hang their head and cry.

But I don't concern myself with that; I took a different vent,
I look forward to what life holds and not what has been spent.
So strap me to the engine as securely as can be,
I want to be on the front to see what I can see.

I want to feel the winds of change blowing in my face,
I want to see what life unfolds as I move from place to place.
I want to see what's coming up, not looking at the past,
Life's too short for yesterdays; it moves along too fast.

So if the ride gets bumpy while you are looking back
Go up front, and you may find your life has jumped the track.
It's all right to remember, that's part of history,
Up front is where it happens, no cause for mystery.

The enjoyment of living is not where we have been,
It's looking ever forward to another year and ten.
It's searching all the byways, never should you refrain,
For if you want to live your life, you gotta drive the train.

✝ Blessing of Thorns ✝

Sandra felt as low as the heels of her shoes as she plodded through a November gust and entered the florist shop. Her life had been like a warm spring breeze, until the fourth month of her second pregnancy when a minor automobile accident stole that from her.

During this Thanksgiving week she would have delivered a son. She grieved over her loss. As if that were not enough, her husband's company threatened a transfer. And her sister, whose holiday visit she coveted, called to say she could not come.

Sandra's friend infuriated her by suggesting her grief was a God-given path to maturity that would allow her to empathize with others who suffer. *She has no idea what I'm feeling*, thought Sandra with a shudder.

Thanksgiving for what?, she wondered. *For a careless driver whose truck was hardly scratched when he rear-ended her? For an airbag that saved her life but took that of her child?*

"Good afternoon, can I help you?" The shop clerk startled her.

"I need an arrangement," stammered Sandra.

"Do you want beautiful but ordinary, or would you like to seize the day with a favorite I call the Thanksgiving Special?" asked the clerk. "I'm convinced that flowers tell stories," she continued. "Are you looking for something that conveys gratitude this Thanksgiving?"

"Not exactly," Sandra blurted. "In the last five months, everything that could go wrong has gone wrong."

Sandra regretted her outburst and was surprised when the shop clerk responded, "I have the perfect arrangement for you."

The shop door's small bell rang, and the clerk greeted, "Hi, Barbara. Let me get your order." She went into a tiny room and reappeared with an arrangement of thorny, long-stemmed roses—except the rose stems were neatly snipped: there were no flowers.

"Want this in a box?" asked the clerk cheerily.

Sandra awaited the customer's response and pondered, *Was this a joke? Who would want rose stems with no flowers?* She expected laughter, but neither woman laughed.

"Yes, please," Barbara replied with an appreciative smile. "You'd think after three years of getting the special, I wouldn't be so moved by its significance. But I feel it right here," as she gently tapped her chest. She left with her order.

"Uh," uttered Sandra, "that lady left with, uh, she left with no flowers."

"Right," said the clerk. "I cut off the flowers. That's the Thanksgiving Thorns Bouquet."

"Oh, come on, you can't tell me people are willing to pay for that," exclaimed Sandra.

"Barbara came into the shop three years ago feeling much like you," explained the clerk. "She thought she had very little to be thankful for. She had lost her father to cancer, the family business was failing, her son was into drugs, and she was facing major surgery.

"That same year I lost my husband," continued the clerk, "and, for the first time in my life, spent the holidays alone. No children, no husband, no family nearby, and too deep in debt to afford travel."

"What did you do?" asked Sandra.

"I learned to be grateful for thorns," said the clerk softly. "I always thanked God for the good things in my life and never questioned them, but when bad stuff hit, did I ever ask questions. It took a while for me to learn that dark times are important. I have always enjoyed the flowers of life, but it took thorns to show me the comfort of God's love. You know, the Bible says that God comforts us when we're afflicted, and from His consolation we learn to comfort others."

Sandra sucked in her breath as she thought about the very thing her best friend had tried to tell her. "I guess the truth is I don't want comfort. I've lost a baby and I'm angry with God."

Then, another person entered. "Hey, Phil," shouted the clerk to the balding, rotund man.

"My wife sent me to pick up our usual Thanksgiving Special, twelve thorny, long-stemmed stems," laughed Phil as the clerk handed him a tissue-wrapped arrangement from the refrigerator.

"Those are for your wife?" asked Sandra incredulously. "Do you mind me asking why she wants a bouquet like that?"

"I'm glad you asked," Phil replied. "Four years ago, my wife and I nearly divorced. After forty years, we were a mess, but with the Lord's grace and guidance, we slogged through problem after problem. He rescued our marriage.

"Jenny (the clerk) told me she kept a vase of rose stems to remind her of what she learned from thorny times. That was good enough for me. I took the stems home and my wife and I labeled each one for a specific problem and gave thanks for what that problem taught us."

As Phil paid the clerk, he encouraged Sandra, "I highly recommend the Special."

"I don't know if I can be thankful for the thorns in my life," Sandra said. "It's too fresh."

The clerk replied thoughtfully, "My experience has shown me that thorns make roses more precious. We value God's providential care more during trouble than at any other time. After all, it was a crown of thorns that Jesus wore so we might know His love. Don't resent the thorns."

Tears rolled down Sandra's cheeks. For the first time since the accident, she loosened her grip on resentment. "I'll take those twelve long-stemmed thorns, please," she managed to choke out.

"I hoped you would," said the clerk gently. "I'll have them ready in a minute."

"Thank you. What do I owe you?"

"Nothing but a promise to allow God to heal your heart. The first year's arrangement is on me." The clerk smiled and handed a card to Sandra. "I'll attach this card to your arrangement, but maybe you would like to read it first."

Sandra read it aloud: "My God, I have never thanked You for my thorns. I have thanked You a thousand times for my roses, but never once for my thorns. Teach me the glory of the cross I bear; teach me the value of my thorns. Show me that I have climbed closer to You along the path of pain. Show me that, through my tears, the colors of Your rainbow look much more brilliant."

✝ Fiery Sermon ✝

A church member, who had attended services regularly, abruptly stopped. The pastor decided to visit him. It was a chilly evening and the pastor found the man alone at home sitting before a blazing fire. Guessing the reason for his pastor's visit, the man led him to a comfortable chair near the fireplace and waited.

The pastor made himself at home but said nothing. In the silence, he contemplated the flames dancing around the burning logs. After a moment, the pastor used the fire tongs to carefully pick up a brightly burning ember and place it to one side of the hearth alone. He sat back in his chair, still silent. The host watched in quiet meditation. As the one lone ember's flame flickered and diminished, there was a momentary glow and its fire was no more. Soon it was cold and dead.

Not a word had been exchanged since the initial greeting. The pastor glanced at his watch and realized it was time to leave. He stood, slowly picked up the dead ember, and placed it back in the middle of the fire. Immediately, it glowed to life with the light and warmth of the burning coals surrounding it.

As the pastor reached the door, his host said with a tear running down his cheek, "Thank you for your visit and especially the fiery sermon. I shall be in church next Sunday."

✟ God Has a Plan for You ✟

Three trees in the forest were discussing their hopes and dreams. The first tree, "I hope to be a treasure chest decorated with intricate carvings and filled with gold, silver, and precious gems. Everyone would see my beauty."

The second tree, "I will be a mighty ship to take kings and queens across waters and sail to the corners of the world. Everyone will feel safe in me because of the strength of my hull."

The third, "I want to be the tallest and straightest tree in the forest. People will see me atop the hill and gaze up to my branches and think how close to God in heaven I reach. I will be the greatest of trees and remembered forever."

After years of the trees praying that their dreams would come true, a group of woodsmen arrived. One came to the first tree and said, "This looks like a strong tree, I should be able to sell the wood to a carpenter." He began cutting it down. The tree was happy, because he knew the carpenter would make him into a treasure chest.

At the second tree, one woodsman said, "This looks like a strong tree. I should be able to sell it to a shipyard." The tree was happy, because he was on his way to becoming a mighty ship.

When the woodsmen came upon the third tree, the tree was afraid, because if cut down, its dream would not come true. One woodsman said, "I don't need anything special from my tree, so I'll take this one." He cut it down, much to the dismay of the tree.

When the first tree arrived at the carpenter's he was made into a feed box for animals, placed in a barn, and filled with hay. This was not quite what he had prayed for.

The second tree was made into a small fishing boat. His dreams of being a mighty ship and carrying kings had come to a dismal end.

The third tree was cut into large pieces and left alone in the dark.

Years went by and the trees forgot their dreams. One day, a man and woman came to the barn. She gave birth and laid the baby in the hay in the feed box that was made from the first tree.

The man wished he could have made a crib for the baby, but this manger would have to do. The tree could feel the importance of the event and knew it held the greatest treasure in history.

Years later, a group of men boarded the fishing boat made from the second tree. One of them was tired and slept. While they were at sea, a great storm arose, and the tree did not think it was strong enough to keep the men safe.

They woke the sleeping man who stood and commanded, "Peace," and the storm ceased. The tree knew it had carried the King of Kings in its boat.

At last, they came for the third tree. It was carried through the streets while the crowd mocked the man dragging it. The man was nailed to the tree and raised in the air to die at the top of a hill.

When Sunday came, the tree realized it was strong enough to stand atop the hill and be as close to God as possible, because Jesus had been crucified on it.

✟ Manufacturer Recall ✟

Regardless of make or year, all units known as "human beings" are being recalled by the Manufacturer. This is due to malfunction in the original prototypes, code-named "Adam" and "Eve," resulting in reproduction of the same defect in all subsequent units.

The defect is technically termed "Serious Internal Non-morality," commonly referred to by the acronym, SIN. Defect symptoms of SIN:

[a] Loss of direction

[b] Lack of peace and joy

[c] Depression

[d] Foul vocal emissions

[e] Selfishness

[f] Ingratitude

[g] Fearfulness

[h] Rebellion

[i] Jealousy

The Manufacturer is providing a factory-authorized repair service free of charge to correct the SIN imperfection. Master Repair Tech Rep, Jesus Christ, has generously offered to bear the entire burden of the staggering cost of the repairs.

To repeat, there is no fee required. The number to call for repair is: P-R-A-Y-E-R (77-2937). Once connected, please upload the burden of SIN through the Repentance procedure. Next, download Atonement from Repair Tech Rep, Christ, into the heart component of the human unit.

No matter how big or small the SIN, Christ will make it whole with:

[a] Love

[b] Joy

[c] Peace

[d] Kindness

[e] Goodness

[f] Faithfulness

[g] Gentleness

[h] Patience

[i] Self-control

Please refer to the operating manual, the Bible, for further details on use of these restorations.

As an upgrade, the Manufacturer has made available to repaired units a facility enabling direct monitoring and assistance from the resident Maintenance Tech Rep, the Holy Spirit. Repaired units need only welcome Him and He will take up residence on the premises.

Warning: Continuing to operate a unit without corrections voids the Manufacturer warranty, exposing the unit to perils too numerous to list, and will ultimately result in incineration of the human being.

Thank you for your immediate attention,

The Manufacturer

⌖ A Mother Asked ⌖

A mother asked President Bush,
"Why did my son have to die in Iraq?"

Another mother asked President Kennedy,
"Why did my son have to die in Viet Nam?"

Another mother asked President Truman,
"Why did my son have to die in Korea?

Another mother asked President F.D. Roosevelt,
"Why did my son have to die at Iwo Jima?"

Another mother asked President W. Wilson,
"Why did my son have to die on a battlefield in France?"

Yet another mother asked President Lincoln,
"Why did my son have to die at Gettysburg?"

And yet another mother asked President Washington,
"Why did my son have to die near Valley Forge?"

Then long, long ago, a mother asked the Heavenly Father,
"Why did my Son have to die on a cross outside of Jerusalem?"

The Father answered: "So that others may have life and dwell in peace, happiness, and freedom."

Only two defining forces have ever offered to die for you:

Jesus Christ and American military personnel.

One died for your soul; the other for your freedom.

✝ Daily Chores ✝

Monday – Washing Day:

Lord, help me wash away my selfishness and vanity, so I may serve you with perfect humility through the week ahead.

Tuesday – Ironing Day:

Dear Lord, help me iron out the wrinkles of prejudice collected through the years, so I may see the beauty in others.

Wednesday – Mending Day:

O God, help me mend my ways, so I will not set a bad example for others.

Thursday – Cleaning Day:

Lord Jesus, help me to dust off the many faults I have been hiding in the secret corners of my heart.

Friday – Shopping Day:

O God, give me the grace to shop wisely, so I may purchase eternal happiness for myself and others in need of love.

Saturday – Cooking Day:

Help me, my Savior, to brew a big kettle of brotherly love and to serve it with the clean, sweet bread of human kindness.

Sunday – The Lord's Day:

O God, I have prepared my house for you. Please come into my heart so I may spend this day and the rest of my life in your presence.

✝ Innocence of a Baby ✝

In the diner, we had the lone table with children. Seating Erik, I noticed a hush overcame the restaurant. Suddenly, Erik squealed gleefully and pounded his stubby fists on the highchair tray. His eyes crinkled with joy, his mouth smiled a toothless grin, and he giggled with gaiety.

I turned to detect the source of his merriment. A man wore baggy pants with a zipper at half-mast and his toes poked out of would-be shoes. His shirt was dirty and hair unkempt; his facial whiskers too short to be considered a beard and a nose so varicose it looked like a road map.

His hands waved and flapped on loose wrists. "Hi there, baby. Hi there, big boy. I see ya, buster," the man goo-gooed to Erik.

My husband and I exchanged a silent plea, *What do we do*? Erik continued to respond.

Every face in the restaurant focused on the old geezer who was creating a scene with my beautiful baby. Our dinner arrived and the man shouted across the room. "Do you patty-cake? Do you peek-a-boo? Hey, look, he knows peek-a-boo."

Nobody thought the old man was cute as he was obviously drunk. My husband and I were embarrassed. We ate in silence while Erik ran through his repertoire for the admiring skid row bum, who reciprocated with loud remarks.

When we finished the meal, my husband went to pay the check and told me to meet him in the parking lot. The old man sat between me and the door. I prayed, "Lord, get me out of here before he speaks to me or Erik."

As I drew closer, I turned my back to sidestep him and avoid any air he might be breathing. But, Erik leaned over my shoulder and reached with open arms to the man.

Before I could grab him, he had propelled himself from my arms to the man's grasp. Instantly, an old stinking man and a young pure baby consummated their love and kinship. In an act of trust, love, and submission, Erik laid his tiny head upon the man's ragged shoulder.

The man's eyes closed tightly and tears hovered below his lashes. His aged hands, full of grime, pain, and hard labor, cradled my baby's bottom and softly stroked his back. I stood paralyzed and awestruck as the old man cradled Erik in his arms.

His eyes opened and set squarely on mine and in a commanding voice, he said, "Take good care of this baby."

Somehow, I uttered from a constricted throat, "I will."

He pried Erik from his chest, lovingly and longingly, as though he were in pain. I received my baby and the man said, "God bless you, ma'am, you've given me my CHRISTmas gift."

I managed a mumbled, "Thanks" and, with Erik in my arms, ran for the car. My husband wondered why I was crying, holding Erik so tightly and entreating, "My God, forgive me."

I had witnessed Christ's love expressed through the innocence of a tiny child who saw no sin nor made any judgment; a child who saw a soul and a mother who saw a suit of clothes. I was a Christian who was blind, holding a child who was not.

I heard God asking, "Are you willing to share your son for a moment?" when He shared His for eternity.

Spiritual Humor e-Soup *A Compilation of Amusing Messages from the Internet*

You Must Be Like Children to Enter the Kingdom

With arms extended toward heaven and a rapturous look on his upturned face, the minister began, "Dear Lord, without you, we are but dust—"

He would have continued had not my very obedient daughter who was listening asked quite audibly in her shrill little girl voice, "Mom, what is butt dust?"

✟ Wherever Love Goes ✟

A woman came out of her house and saw three old men with long white beards sitting in her yard. Not recognizing them, she said, "I don't think I know you but you must be hungry. Please, come in and have something to eat."

"Is the man of the house home?" they asked.

"No," she replied.

"Then we cannot come in," they replied.

In the evening when her husband came home, she told him what had happened.

"Go tell them I'm home and invite them in." The woman went and invited the men in.

"We do not go into a house together," they replied.

"Why is that?" she asked.

One old man explained: "His name is Wealth," pointing to one, "he is Success," pointing to the other. "And, I am Love." He added, "Ask your husband which one you want in your home."

The woman told her husband what was said. He was overjoyed. "How nice, we'll invite Wealth. Let him in and fill our home with wealth."

His wife disagreed, "Dear, why don't we invite Success?"

Their daughter-in-law, listening from the other side of the house, made a suggestion: "Wouldn't it be better to invite Love to fill our home with love."

"Let's heed our daughter-in-law's advice," said the husband. "Invite Love to be our guest."

The woman asked the men, "Which of you is Love? Please, come in and be our guest."

Love walked toward the house followed by the other two. Surprised, the lady asked Wealth and Success, "I invited Love, why are you coming?"

The three replied in unison, "If you had invited either Wealth or Success, the other two of us would've stayed out. Since you invited Love, wherever He goes, we go."

✟ A Living Bible ✟

Bill wears wild hair, a T-shirt with holes in it, jeans, and no shoes: his wardrobe for four years of college. He is brilliant, eclectic, and unpretentious. He became a Christian while in college.

Across the street from campus is a stylish but conservative church that wants to minister to students but is not sure how to proceed. One day, Bill attends the church while a service is in progress and walks down the aisle seeking a seat. The pews are packed and no seat is open. People become uncomfortable with this stranger but nothing is said. Nearing the pulpit and realizing there is no seat available, he squats down on the carpet.

Although perfectly acceptable behavior at college fellowship, nothing like this has happened in this church before. The assembly becomes more uneasy and the tension in the air is palpable.

A silver-haired deacon using his cane ambles up the aisle. The deacon, in his eighties and wearing an elegant three-piece suit, is a godly man, dignified and courtly. As he nears Bill, everyone knows the intruder will get what he deserves. How can the deacon, a man of his age and background, accept a college kid sitting on the floor of the church during worship services?

The church is silent except for the clicking of the deacon's cane. All eyes focus on him. The minister stops preaching until the deacon does his duty.

To everyone's astonishment, the elderly man drops his cane on the floor and, with difficulty, lowers himself next to Bill and accompanies him in his worship.

The congregation chokes up with emotion. The minister gains control and proclaims, "What I'm about to preach, you will never remember. What you have seen, you will never forget."

Be careful how you live. You may be the only Bible some people will ever read.

✟ Don't Dance So Fast ✟

Have you ever watched kids on a merry-go-round?
Or listened to the rain slapping on the ground?
Ever followed a butterfly's erratic flight
Or gazed at the sun into the fading night?
You'd better slow down, don't dance so fast.
Time is short, the music won't last.

Do you run through each day on the fly?
When you ask, "How are you?" do you hear the reply?
When the day is done, do you lie in your bed
With the next hundred chores running through your head?
You'd better slow down, don't dance so fast.
Time is short, the music won't last.

Ever told your child, "We'll do it tomorrow,"
And in your haste, not seen his sorrow?
Ever lost touch, let a good friendship die
'Cause you never had time to call and say, "Hi"?
You'd better slow down, don't dance so fast.
Time is short, the music won't last.

When you run so fast to get somewhere,
You miss half the fun of getting there.
When you worry and hurry through your day,
It is like an unopened gift thrown away.
Life is not a race. Do take it slower.
Hear the music before the song is over.

✟ Highway 109 ✟

A drunk in an Oldsmobile had run the light
That caused the pileup on 109 that night.
Broken bodies lay about with blood everywhere,
The sirens screamed elegies, for death was in the air.

A mother, trapped inside her car, was heard above the noise.
Her plaintive plea near split the air, "Oh, please, God, spare my boys."
She fought to loose her hands and struggled to get free.
But mangled metal gripped her fast in grim captivity.

Her frightened eyes focused where the back seat once had been.
But all she saw was broken glass and two children's seats crushed in.
Her twins were nowhere to be seen, she did not hear them cry,
She prayed they'd been thrown free, "Oh, God, don't let them die."

Firemen cut her loose, but when they searched the back,
They found no little boys, just their seat belts intact.
They thought the woman had gone mad and was traveling alone.
They turned to question her and discovered she was gone.

Policemen saw her running wild and screaming above the noise
In beseeching supplication, "Please help me find my boys.
They're four-year-olds, wearing blue shirts and jeans to match."
A cop spoke up, "They're in my car, and they don't have a scratch.

"They said their daddy put them there and gave them each a cone,
And told them both to wait for Mom to come and take them home.
I've searched the area high and low, but cannot find their dad.
He must have fled the scene, I guess, and that is very bad."

The mother hugged the twins and said, while wiping at a tear,
"He couldn't flee the scene, you see, for he's been dead a year."
The cop looked confused and asked, "Now, how can that be true?"
The boys said, "Mommy, Daddy came and left a kiss for you.

"He told us not to worry and that you would be all right,
And then he put us in this car with the pretty, flashing light.
We wanted him to stay with us, because we miss him so,
But Mommy, he just hugged us tight and said he had to go."

"He said someday we'd understand and told us not to fuss,
And he said to tell you, Mommy, he's watching over us."
The mother knew without a doubt that what they spoke was true,
For she recalled their dad's last words, "I'll be watching over you."

The firemen's notes could not explain the twisted, mangled car,
And how the three of them escaped without a single scar.
But on the cop's report was scribed, in print so very fine,
"An angel walked the beat tonight on highway 109."

✟ Angel at the Door ✟

There came a frantic knock at the doctor's office door,
A knock more urgent than he'd ever heard before.
"Come in, come in," the impatient doctor said,
"Come in, come in, before you wake the dead."

In walked a frightened little girl, a child no more than nine.
It was plain for all to see, she had troubles on her mind.

"Oh doctor, I beg you, please come with me,
My mother's surely dying, she's as sick as she can be."

"I don't make house calls, bring your mother here."
"But she's too sick, so you must come or she will die I fear."
The doctor, touched by her devotion, decided he would go,
She said he would be blessed, more than he could know.

She led him to her house where her mother lay in bed,
Her mother was so very sick she couldn't raise her head.
But her eyes cried out for help and help her the doctor did,
She would have died that very night if not for her kid.

The doctor got her fever down and she lived through the night,
And morning brought the doctor signs that she would be all right.
The doctor said he had to leave but would return by two,
And later he came back to check, like he said he'd do.

The mother praised the doctor for all the things he'd done,
He told her she would've died, were it not for her little one.
"How proud you must be of your wonderful little girl,
It was her pleading that made me come, she's really quite a pearl."

"But doctor, my daughter died over three years ago,
Is the picture on the wall of the little girl you know?"
The doctor's legs went limp, for the picture on the wall
Was the same little girl for whom he'd made this call.

The doctor stood motionless for quite a little while,
And then his solemn face was broken by his smile.
He was thinking of that frantic knock heard at his office door,
And of the beautiful little angel that had walked across his floor.

✝ God's Oath ✝

When you are sad I will dry your tears.
When you are scared I will comfort your fears.
When you are worried I will give you hope.
When you are confused I will help you cope.

When you are lost and can't see the light
I shall be your beacon shining ever so bright.
This is my oath I pledge till the end.
Why you may ask? Because you're my friend.

✝ My Wish for You ✝

I wish you a day of ordinary miracles:
A fresh pot of coffee you didn't have to make yourself,
An unexpected phone call from an old friend,
Green traffic lights on your way to work.

I wish you a day of little things to rejoice in:
The fastest line at the grocery store,
A good singalong song on the radio,
Your keys right where you look.

I wish you a day of happiness and perfection:
Bite-size pieces of perfection,
The knowledge that the Lord is smiling on you,
The comfortable feeling the Lord is holding you because you are special.

I wish you a day of peace and joy in Him.

⌖ Puppy Size ⌖

"Danielle repeats it over and over. We've been back to this animal shelter at least five times and it's been weeks since we started," the mother told the volunteer.

"What is it she keeps asking for?" the volunteer inquired.

"Puppy size," replied the mother.

"Well, we have plenty of puppies, if that's what she's looking for."

"I know. We've seen most of them," the mom said in frustration.

Danielle walked into the office.

"Well, did you find one?" asked her mom.

"No, not this time," Danielle said with sadness in her voice. "Can we come back on the weekend?" The two women shook their heads and laughed.

"Never know when we'll get more dogs. Unfortunately, there's always a supply," the volunteer said.

Danielle took her mother's hand and headed to the door. "Don't worry, I'll find one this weekend," she said.

Over the next days, Mom and Dad had long conversations with her. They felt she was being too particular. Dad finally laid down the law, "It's this weekend or we're not looking any more."

"We don't want to hear anything more about puppy size either," Mom added.

Sure enough, they were first in the shelter on Saturday. Danielle ran straight to the section that housed the smaller dogs.

Tired of the routine, mom sat in the waiting room where there was a window to observe the animals. Danielle walked slowly from cage to cage, kneeling periodically to take a closer look. One by one, the dogs were brought out and she held each one.

One by one, she said, "Sorry, you're not the one."

At the last cage on the last day of the search for the perfect pup, a volunteer opened the door and Danielle tenderly picked up the dog and held it closely. This examination took a little longer.

"Mom, I found the puppy. He's the one. I know it. It's the puppy size," she squealed in joy.

"He's the same size as the other puppies," Mom said.

"Not size; sighs. When I held him, he sighed. Don't you remember when I asked you what love is? You said love depends on the sighs of your heart; the more you love, the bigger the sighs."

She stooped to hug her child but did not know whether to laugh or cry; she did a bit of both.

"Mom, when you hold me, I sigh. When you and Daddy hug each other, you sigh. I knew I would find the right puppy if it sighed when I held it," she said. Holding the puppy close to her face, she said, "He loves me, Mom. I heard the sighs of his heart."

✟ Lost Geese: A CHRISTmas Parable ✟

There was a man who did not believe in God, the incarnation, or the spiritual meaning of CHRISTmas. His wife was a devout believer and diligently raised her children in the faith. He often gave her a hard time and mocked her religious observance of CHRISTmas.

One snowy CHRISTmas Eve, she was taking the kids to church service. She pleaded with him to come, but he refused and ridiculed the idea of Christ's incarnation. "Why would God lower himself and become human like us? That's ridiculous."

After they left, the winds picked up and the snowfall turned into a blizzard. As he sat down to relax by the fire, he heard a thump, something hitting the window, and another. He peered out but could not see, so he ventured outside to get a better look.

He saw the strangest sight: a flock of geese. Apparently, flying to warmer weather, they got caught in the storm, which had become too violent for them to fly. They were stranded on his farm with no food or shelter. They flew blindly in circles around his field.

Compassion compelled him to consider, "The barn would be a great place for them. It's warm and safe. They could spend the night and wait out the storm." He opened the doors and waited for the geese to notice and fly inside. But they continued to flutter aimlessly, ignoring the safety of the barn.

He whistled and signaled, shouted, jumped up and down, and waved his arms. But they did not pay attention. He moved closer, but they fearfully moved away. He went to the house, returned with bread, and made a trail leading to the barn. They still did not get it.

He tried to herd them into the barn but succeeded only to scare and scatter them, in every direction except the barn. Nothing he did could get them to enter the safety and shelter of the barn, the one place where they could survive.

Frustrated, he exclaimed, "Why don't they listen to me? Why don't they follow me? What's wrong with them? Can't they see this is the only place they can survive? How can I get them into the one place that can save them?"

Finally, he realized they will not follow a human and pondered, *If I became like them, I could show them the way and save them. They would follow me, not fear me. They would trust me and I could lead them to safety.*

He stood silently as the words reverberated in his mind: If I became like them, I could show them the way and save them. He recalled what he said to his wife: Why would God lower himself and become human like us? That's ridiculous.

Something in his mind clicked as he put these two together: a revelation, he understood the incarnation. We were like the geese: blind, gone astray, and perishing. God became like us so He could show us the way and save us. That is the meaning of CHRISTmas, he realized in his heart.

As the winds and blinding snow abated, his heart quieted and he contemplated this epiphany. He understood what CHRISTmas was about. He knew why Christ had come. Years of doubt and disbelief were shattered, as he humbly and tearfully knelt down in the snow and embraced the true meaning of CHRISTmas.

☩ Dinner and a Movie ☩

After twenty-one years of marriage, my wife wanted me to take another woman to dinner and a movie. "I love you, but I know this other woman loves you and would like to spend time with you." The "other" woman was my mother, who had been a widow for years. The demands of my work and our family made it possible to visit her only infrequently.

I called to invite her for dinner and a movie. "What's wrong, are you well?" she gasped, being the type of woman who suspects a late-night call or surprise invitation as a sign of bad news.

"I thought it would be pleasant to spend some time with you," I responded.

She thought about it and replied, "I would like that very much."

Friday evening, driving to pick her up, I was nervous. Arriving at her home, I noticed that she, too, seemed anxious about our date. She waited in the door with her coat on. She had curled her hair and wore the dress she had celebrated her last wedding anniversary in.

Her face beamed an angelic smile. "I told my friends I had a date with my son; they were impressed," she pronounced proudly, entering the car. "They can't wait to hear about our date."

We went to a restaurant that, although not elegant, was nice and cozy. Mom took my arm as if she were the First Lady. After we sat down, I read the menu since she could not read small print. Halfway through the entrées, I glanced up and noticed Mom staring at me.

A nostalgic grin appeared as she joshed. "I used to have to read the menu for you years ago."

"I'm glad I can return the favor," I responded.

During dinner, we had an agreeable conversation, catching up on recent events of each other's life. We talked so much we missed the movie. Later, as we arrived at her house, she offered, "I'll go out with you again, but only if you let me invite you." I joyfully agreed.

"How was your dinner date?" asked my wife when I returned.

"Very nice, much more than I could have imagined," I answered.

Not long after, my mother died of a heart attack. It happened so suddenly I did not have a chance to do anything for her.

Weeks later, I received a letter with a gift certificate from the restaurant where mother and I had dined. A note stated: "I paid the bill in advance since I wasn't sure I could be there. I bought two dinners: for you and your wife. You will never know what that night meant for me. I love you, son."

In that instant, I understood the importance of saying, "I love you," and giving our loved ones the time they deserve. Nothing in life is more important than your family. Give them your attention, because these things cannot be put off till you "have the time."

✠ The King's Insurance Company ✠

Guarantees

Life: For God so loved the world that He gave His only begotten Son, that whoever believes in Him shall not perish but have everlasting life. John 3:16

Health: Who forgives all the iniquities, who heals all your diseases? Psalm 103:3

Clothing: If the God so clothes the grass, which today is in the field and tomorrow is thrown into the oven, how much will He clothe you? Luke 12:28

Daily Needs: And my God shall supply all your need according to His riches in glory by Christ Jesus. Philippians 4:19

Comfort: Let not your heart be troubled; you believe in God, believe also in Me. John 14:1

Companionship: Teaching them to observe all things that I have commanded you; and lo, I am with you always, even to the end of the age. Matthew 28:20

Peace: Peace I leave with you; my peace I give to you; not as the world gives do I give to you. Let not your heart be troubled, neither let it be afraid. John 14:27

An Eternal Home: In my Father's house are many mansions; if it were not so, I would have told you. I go to prepare a place for you. John 14:2

Reasons for insuring with The King's Insurance Company

1. The oldest insurance company in the world.
2. The only insurance company underwriting against loss in the Judgment Day fire.
3. The only insurance company that provides eternal coverage.
4. The policy never changes.
5. Management never changes.
6. Assets too vast to measure.
7. The only insurance company that pays the premium.

Policy

But God demonstrates His own love toward us, in that while we were still sinners, Christ died for us. Romans 5:8

For by grace you have been saved through faith; and that not of yourselves, it is the gift of God. Ephesians 2:8

For you were bought at a price; therefore glorify God in your body and in your Spirit, which are God's. 1 Corinthians 6:20

Application Procedure

That if you confess with your mouth the Lord Jesus and believe in your heart that God has raised Him from the dead, you will be saved. Romans 10:9

For whosoever calls on the name of the Lord shall be saved. Romans 10:13

Premium

All premiums have been paid in full by Jesus Christ.

✟ What Is Happiness? ✟

A ninety-two-year-old man, fully dressed by 8 A.M. each day with his hair neatly combed and face perfectly shaved, even though legally blind, moved to a nursing home.

His wife of seventy years had recently passed away, necessitating the move. After waiting patiently in the lobby, he smiled sweetly when told his room was ready. As he maneuvered his walker to the elevator, I provided a visual description of his room, including the eyelet window curtains.

"I love it," he stated with the enthusiasm of a child having been presented with a new puppy.

"Mr. Jones, you haven't seen the room yet."

"That doesn't have anything to do with it," he replied. "Happiness is something you decide on ahead of time. Whether I like my room or not doesn't depend on how the furniture is arranged, it's how I arrange my mind. I already decided to love it.

"It's a decision I make every morning. I have a choice: I can spend the day in bed recounting the difficulty I have with parts of my body that no longer work, or get out of bed and be thankful for the ones that do.

"Each day is a gift. As long as my eyes open, I'll focus on the new day and happy memories I've stored away especially for this time in my life.

"Old age is like a bank account. You withdraw from it what you've put in. My advice is to deposit a lot of happiness in the bank account of memories.

"Thank you for your part in adding to my memory bank. I'm still depositing."

✟ The Brick ✟

A young, successful executive was cruising down a neighborhood street in his new Jaguar. He was watching for kids darting out from between parked cars and slowed when he thought he saw something.

As his car passed, no children appeared. Instead, a brick smashed into the Jag's door. He slammed on the brakes and backed the Jag to the spot where the brick had come.

The angry driver jumped from the car, grabbed the nearest kid, pushed him against a car and shouted, "What was that all about and who are you? That's a new car and the brick you threw is going to cost a lot of money. Why did you do it?"

The young boy apologized, "Please, mister, please, I'm sorry but I didn't know what else to do." He pleaded, "I threw the brick because no one else would stop."

With tears running down his face, he pointed to a spot around a parked car. "It's my brother," he said. "He rolled off the curb and fell out of his wheelchair and I can't lift him up."

Sobbing, the boy asked the stunned executive, "Please, can you help me get him back into his wheelchair? He's too heavy for me."

Moved beyond words, the driver swallowed the rapidly swelling lump in his throat. He handily lifted the handicapped boy back into the wheelchair and dabbed his handkerchief at the fresh scrapes and cuts. A quick assessment assured him everything was going to be okay.

"Thank you and may God bless you," the grateful child told the stranger. Too shaken to speak, the man could only watch the boy push his wheelchair-bound brother down the sidewalk.

It was a long, slow walk back to the Jaguar. The damage was very noticeable but the driver never repaired it. He kept the dent to remind him of the message, "Don't go through life so fast that God has to throw a brick at you to get your attention."

Why Didn't You Warn Me?

The sheriff drove his SUV through the heavy rains to the isolated home of John Smith. Mr. Smith met him on the front porch with an umbrella over his head. The sheriff warned, "John, flash floods are expected so I came to take you to safety."

Mr. Smith, a God-fearing man, replied, "Thanks, Sheriff, but I'm awaitin' God's warning. He'll tell me when it's time to leave."

"Okay, John, but I wish you'd accompany me in my SUV to safety," said the sheriff, who drove back to town and high ground.

Hours later, the sheriff steered his motorboat through flood waters to the Smith home. Mr. Smith greeted him from his second-story window.

The sheriff pleaded, "John, you can see how bad it is and it's gonna get worse. Let me pick you up in my boat and take you to safety."

Mr. Smith replied, "Thanks, Sheriff, but I'm still awaitin' God's warning. I know he'll take care of me."

Frustrated, the sheriff replied, "John, the next time will be the last time I can help you." He turned the motorboat around and returned to the safety of the town.

Hours later, the sheriff flew his helicopter through the heavy rains above the rough, rising water to John's place. Mr. Smith waved to him with one hand while the other hand grasped the antenna on the top of his roof.

Exasperated, the sheriff demanded, "John, this is your last chance. Let me lower the life hook to you so I can lift you off your roof and fly you to safety."

John replied, "Thanks, Sheriff, but I'm still awaitin' God's warning. I have faith that he is watching out for me."

At wits' end, the sheriff said, "John, I can't do anything else for you so I'm returning to town to batten down the hatches in my office and goin' home to wait out this storm."

The rains continued unabated through the night and washed John Smith from his tenuous hold on the antenna and drowned him in the swift, rushing waters.

Arriving at the gates of heaven, he demanded to speak with God. When God arrived, he complained vehemently, "Why did you let me drown? I waited faithfully for you to warn me when it was time to leave."

God, in a sympathetic voice, responded, "John, my son, I came by three times but you ignored my warnings."

⸸ You Always Know What's Best ⸸

I'm writing to say I'm sorry for being angry yesterday
When you ignored my prayer and things didn't go my way.

First, my car broke down. I was very late for work.
But I missed that awful accident. Was that your handiwork?

I found a house I loved but others got there first.
I was angry, then relieved, when I heard the pipes had burst.

Yesterday, I found the perfect dress but the color was too pale.
Today, I found the dress in red. Would you believe, on sale?

I know you're watching over me and I'm feeling truly blest.
For no matter what I pray for, you always know what's best.

⸸ I Had Lunch with God ⸸

A little boy desired to meet God. He knew it was a long journey, so he packed his bag with cupcakes and soda and set out on his adventure.

When he had traveled three blocks, he met an elderly man sitting in the park feeding pigeons. The boy sat next to him and opened his suitcase. About to drink his soda, he noticed the man looked hungry, so he offered him a cupcake.

The man accepted and smiled a smile so gracious the boy wanted to see it again. So, he offered him a soda. The man smiled again and delighted the boy. They sat together eating and smiling without speaking a word.

As it grew dark, the boy became tired and got up to leave. After a few steps, he ran back to the man and hugged him. The man gave him his biggest smile ever.

When the boy returned home, his mother noticed the joy on his face and asked, "What made you so happy today?"

He said, "I had lunch with God and He's got the most beautiful smile I've ever seen."

Meanwhile, the elderly man, radiant with joy, returned home. His son was surprised by the look of peace on his face and asked, "Dad, what made you so happy today?"

He replied, "I had lunch with God and, you know, he's much younger than I expected."

✟ America the Beautiful ✟

America the Beautiful
Or so you used to be.
Land of the Pilgrims' pride,
I'm glad they'll never see.

Babies piled in dumpsters,
Abortion on demand,
Oh, sweet land of liberty,
Your house is on the sand.

Our children wander aimlessly,
Poisoned by cocaine,
Choosing to indulge their lusts,
When God has said abstain.

From sea to shining sea,
Our nation turns away
From the teaching of God's love
And a need to always pray.

We've kept God in our temples,
how callous we have grown.
When earth is but His footstool,
and Heaven is His throne.

We've voted in a government
That's rotting at the core,
Appointing godless judges
who throw reason out the door.

Too soft to place a killer
In a well-deserved tomb,
But brave enough to kill a babe
Before he leaves the womb.

You think that God's not angry
That our land's a moral slum?
How much longer will He wait
Before His judgment comes?

How are we to face our God,
From Whom we cannot hide?
What then is left for us to do,
But stem this evil tide?

If we who are His children
Will humbly turn and pray,
Seek His holy face,
And mend our evil way,

Then God will hear from Heaven
And forgive us all of our sins,
He'll heal our sickly land
And those who live within.

But, America the Beautiful,
If you don't, then you will see
A sad but Holy God
Withdraw His hand from thee.

⌖ Mean Moms ⌖

I loved you enough to ask where you were going, with whom, and what time you would be home.

I loved you enough to be silent and let you discover that your new best friend was a creep.

I loved you enough to stand over you for two hours while you cleaned your room, a job that should have taken fifteen minutes.

I loved you enough to let you see anger, disappointment, and tears in my eyes. Children must learn that their parents are not perfect.

I loved you enough to let you assume the responsibility for your actions, even when the penalties were so harsh they broke my heart.

But most of all, I loved you enough to say, "No," when I knew you would hate me for it.

Those were the toughest battles of all and I am glad I won, because in the end, you won, too.

When your kids complain about how mean you are, you will retort with pride:

> We had the meanest mom in the whole world.
>
> While other kids ate candy for breakfast, we had cereal, eggs, and toast.
>
> When others had soda and cookies for lunch, we had sandwiches.
>
> Our mom fixed dinner that was different from what other kids had, too.
>
> Our mom insisted on knowing where we were at all times, like we were convicts in a prison.
>
> She had to know who our friends were and what we were doing with them.
>
> She expected if we said we would be gone for an hour, we would be gone for an hour or less.
>
> We were ashamed to admit it but she had the nerve to break child labor laws by making us work.

We had to wash dishes, make beds, learn to cook, vacuum, do laundry, empty trash, and all sorts of cruel jobs.

I think she would lie awake at night thinking of more things for us to do.

She always insisted on us telling the truth, the whole truth, and nothing but the truth.

By the time we were teenagers; she could read our minds and had eyes in the back of her head. Then, life got really tough.

Mom would not let our friends get away with honking the horn when they drove up. They had to come to the door so she could meet them.

While everyone else could date when they were twelve or thirteen, we had to wait until we were ready for marriage.

Because of our mom, we missed lots of things others experienced. None of us have been caught shoplifting, vandalizing others' property, or been arrested for any crime. It was all her fault.

We left home as educated, honest adults.

We are doing our best to be mean parents exactly like Mom was.

I think that is what is wrong with the world. It does not have enough mean moms.

✢ Senior Version of "Jesus Loves Me" ✢

While watching TV on Sunday instead of going to church, I witnessed a congregation honor one of its senior pastors who had been retired many years. He was ninety-two years old and I wondered why they bothered the old gentleman to preach at that age.

After introduction of this speaker and as applause quieted, he rose from his high-back chair and walked with great effort in a sliding gait to the podium. He placed both hands on the pulpit to steady himself and, without a note or reference of any kind, softly spoke.

"When I was invited to talk to you on this occasion, your pastor asked me to tell you what was the greatest lesson ever learned in my fifty-odd years of preaching. I thought about it a few days and boiled it down to one belief that made the greatest difference in my life and sustained me through my trials. The one truth I could always rely on when tears, heartbreak, pain, fear, and sorrow paralyzed me, the certainty that would comfort me, was this verse:

"Jesus loves me this I know.
For the Bible tells me so.
Little ones to him belong,
We are weak but he is strong.
Yes, Jesus loves me,
The Bible tells me so."

When he finished, the church was so silent you could hear his footsteps as he shuffled back to his chair.

A pastor observed, "I noticed it was the adults who always chose the children's hymn 'Jesus Loves Me' (for the children, of course) during a hymn-sing, and it was the adults who sang the loudest because I could see they knew it the best."

Here is a new version for us who have white hair or no hair at all:

Jesus loves me, this I know,
Though my hair is white as snow.
Though my sight is growing dim,
Still He bids me trust in Him.
(Chorus)
Yes, Jesus loves me, yes, Jesus loves me,
Yes, Jesus loves me, for the Bible tells me so.

Though my steps are oh, so slow,
With my hand in His I'll go.
On through life, let come what may,
He'll be there to lead the way.
(Chorus)
Though I am no longer young,
I have much which He's begun.
Let me serve Christ with a smile,
Go with others the extra mile.
(Chorus)
When the nights are dark and long,
In my heart He puts a song.

Telling me in words so clear,
"Have no fear, for I am near."
(Chorus)
When my work on earth is done,
And life's victories have been won.
He will take me home above,
Then I'll understand His love.
(Chorus)
I love Jesus, does he know?
Have I ever told Him so?
Jesus loves to hear me say
That I love Him every day.

✟ Influential Stranger in Our Home ✟

Before I was born, my dad met a stranger who was new to our small town. From the start, Dad was captivated by the newcomer and invited him to live in our home. The stranger was quickly accepted and at hand to welcome me into the world a few months later.

Growing up, I never questioned his special niche in our family. My parents were complementary instructors: Mom taught me the word of God and Dad taught me to obey it.

But the stranger? He was our storyteller. He kept us spellbound endlessly with adventures, mysteries, and comedies. If I wanted to know anything about politics, history, or science, he always knew the answers about the past, understood the present, and even seemed able to predict the future. He took my family to our first major league ballgame. He made me laugh and he made me cry. The stranger never stopped talking but Dad did not seem to mind.

At times, Mom would leave quietly while the rest of us were shushing each other to listen to what he had to say. She would go to her room and read. (I wonder if she ever prayed for the stranger to leave.)

Dad ruled our household with certain moral convictions but the stranger never felt obligated to honor them. For example, profanity from us, friends, or visitors was not allowed in our home. However, our longtime visitor got away with four-letter words that burned my ears, made my dad squirm, and my mother blush.

My dad, a teetotaler, did not permit alcohol in the home, not even for cooking. But the stranger regularly encouraged us to try it. He made cigarettes look cool, cigars manly, and pipes distinguished.

He talked freely, much too freely, about sex with comments that were sometimes blatant, suggestive, and, generally, embarrassing. I realize that my early concepts about relationships were influenced strongly by the stranger. Time after time, he opposed the values of my parents; yet, he was seldom rebuked and never asked to leave.

Fifty years have passed since the stranger moved in with my family. He has blended right in and is not nearly as fascinating as he was at first. Still, if you were to walk into my parents' den today you would find him sitting in his corner, waiting for someone to listen to him talk and watch him exhibit his pictures.

His name? We call him "TV" for short.

✟ My Name Is Rose ✟

The first day of classes our professor introduced himself and asked us to get to know someone we did not already know. I stood up to peer around when a gentle hand touched my shoulder. I turned to find a wrinkled, little old lady beaming at me with a smile that lit up her entire being.

She said, "Hi, handsome. My name is Rose and I'm eighty-seven. Can I give you a hug?"

I laughed and responded enthusiastically, "Of course you may." She gave me a giant squeeze. "Why are you in college at such a young, innocent age?" I queried.

She joked, "I'm here to meet a rich husband, get married, and have a couple of kids."

"No, seriously?" I insisted, curious to know what motivated her to take this hurdle at her age.

"I always dreamed of having a college education and I'm getting one at last," she told me.

After class, we walked to the student union and shared a chocolate milkshake and became instant friends. Every day for the next three months, we would leave class and talk nonstop. I was mesmerized by this "time machine" as she shared her wisdom and experience with me.

Over the course of the year, Rose made friends easily and became a campus icon. She loved to dress up and reveled in the attention bestowed upon her from the other students. She was living it up.

At semester's end, we invited her to speak at our football banquet. I will never forget what she taught us. As she began to deliver her prepared speech, she dropped her notecards on the floor. Frustrated and embarrassed, she leaned into the microphone and said, "I'm sorry I'm so jittery. I gave up beer for Lent and this whiskey is killing me. I'll never get my speech back in order so let me tell you what I know."

As we laughed hysterically, she cleared her throat and began, "We do not stop playing because we are old; we grow old because we stop playing. There are a few secrets to staying young, being happy, and achieving success.

"Laugh and find humor every day. You've got to have a dream. When you lose your dreams, you die. We have so many people walking around who are dead and don't even know it.

"There's a huge difference between growing older and growing up. If you're nineteen and lie in bed for a full year and don't do one productive thing, you will turn twenty. If I am eighty-seven-years old and stay in bed for a year and never do anything, I will still turn eighty-eight.

"Anybody can grow older. That doesn't take any talent or ability. The idea is to grow up by always finding opportunity in change. Have no regrets. The elderly usually don't have regrets for what we did, but rather for what we didn't do. The people who fear death are those with regrets."

She concluded her speech by courageously singing "The Rose." She challenged each of us to study the lyrics and live them out in our daily lives.

At year's end, Rose finished the college degree she had begun years ago.

A week after graduation, Rose died peacefully in her sleep. More than two thousand students attended her funeral in tribute to the wonderful woman who taught by example that it is never too late to be all you can possibly be.

Spiritual Humor e-Soup   *A Compilation of Amusing Messages from the Internet*

Which Hymn Would You Pick?

A pastor reluctantly informed the congregation that the church was in need of money. He asked them to prayerfully consider putting a little extra in the offering. He offered that whoever gave the most would be able to choose three of their favorite hymns.

After the collection, the pastor noted joyfully that someone had donated one thousand dollars. Immediately sharing his joy with the assembly, he said he wanted to personally thank the generous member.

An elderly saintly lady shyly raised her hand and the pastor invited her to the altar. He congratulated her on her charity and, in thanksgiving, asked her to pick her three hymns.

Her face brightened as she peered over the gathering and pointed to the three handsomest men and repeated, "I pick him and him and him."

✟ Morning Prayer ✟

You are ushering in another day untouched and freshly new,
so here I come to ask You God if You'll renew me too?
God, forgive the many errors that I made yesterday
and let me try again, dear God, to walk closer in thy Way.
But Father, I am well aware I can't make it on my own.
So take my hand and hold it tight, for I can't walk alone.

Spiritual Humor e-Soup *A Compilation of Amusing Messages from the Internet*

Dear Lord,

So far today, I'm doing all right. I have not gossiped, lost my temper, been greedy, grumpy, nasty, selfish, or self-indulgent. I have not whined, complained, cursed, or eaten any chocolate. I have charged nothing on my credit card.

But I will be getting out of bed in a minute, and I think I will really need your help then.

⌖ What Goes Around Comes Around ⌖

He almost missed the lady stranded on the side of the road. In the dim light, he could tell she needed help. He pulled in front of her classy car and got out. His jalopy sputtered as he approached her.

Although he wore a friendly smile, she was afraid. No one had stopped to help since her car broke down over an hour ago. Was he going to hurt her? He did not look safe; he looked poor and hungry.

He could tell she was frightened. Standing alone in the cold can put fear in you. He comforted, "I'm here to help you, ma'am. Why don't you wait in your car where it's warm? By the way, my name is Bryan Anderson."

She had a flat tire, but for an elderly woman that was big trouble. He crawled under the car to locate a slot for the jack and skinned his knuckles. Changing the tire, he got dirty and hurt his hands tightening the lug nuts.

After he closed her trunk, she rolled down the window and spoke. "I can't find words to thank you enough. How much do I owe?" Any amount was a small price to pay; she had imagined all that could have befallen her had he not stopped.

Being paid had not entered his mind. He was helping someone in need and, God knows, there were many who lent him a hand in the past. "If you want to pay me, the next time you see someone in need, help them." He added, "And think of me."

Bryan waited until she drove off, her lights disappearing into the night. It had been a cold and depressing day but he felt uplifted as he headed for home.

A mile down the road, the lady saw a small diner. She stopped to eat and take the chill off before she made the last leg of her trip. Two obsolete gas pumps stood sentinel to the old, dingy restaurant, a scene unfamiliar to her.

Inside, the waitress greeted her with a clean towel to dry her hair. She offered a sweet smile even after being on her feet the whole day. The lady noticed she was nearly eight months pregnant but did not let the aches and strain affect her attitude. The lady wondered, *How can someone who has so little be so kind to a stranger*? Then, she remembered Bryan.

After finishing her meal, she paid with a hundred-dollar bill. As the waitress went for change, the old lady covertly slipped out the door and was gone by the time the waitress returned.

The waitress wondered where the lady could be. She noticed the writing on the napkin. Tears dampened her eyes as she read the message: "You don't owe me any change; I've been there. Somebody once helped me the way I'm helping you. If you want to repay me, do not let this circle of love end with you." Hidden under the napkin were four more hundred-dollar bills.

There were tables to clear, sugar bowls to fill and customers to serve, but the waitress made it through another day. When she returned home and climbed into bed, she was thinking about the money and the lady's request. How could the lady have known how much she and her husband needed the financial aid? With the baby due next month, it would be difficult.

She knew how her husband worried. As he lay asleep next to her, she kissed him softly and whispered, "Everything's going to be okay. I love you, Bryan Anderson."

✟ Map ✟

A father wanted to read a magazine but was being disturbed by his little girl, Shelby. She wanted to know what the United States looked like. He removed a sheet from his magazine on which was printed the map of the country.

Ripping the map into small pieces and handing them to Shelby, he said, "Go into the other room and see if you can put this together."

After a few minutes, she returned with the map correctly pieced together. The father was surprised and asked how she had finished so quickly.

She answered, "On the other side of the paper is a picture of Jesus. When I put Jesus back where He belonged, our country came together naturally.

Spiritual Humor e-Soup — *A Compilation of Amusing Messages from the Internet*

Giving When It Counts

I worked as a hospital volunteer and got to know a little girl suffering from a rare disease. Her only chance of recovery appeared to be a blood transfusion from her five-year-old brother. He had miraculously survived the disease and developed the antibodies needed to combat the illness.

The doctor explained the situation and asked him if he would be willing to give his blood to his sister. He hesitated a moment before taking a deep breath and agreeing, "I'll do it if it will save my sister."

During the transfusion, he lay in bed next to his sister and smiled, as we all did, seeing the color returning to her cheek. Abruptly, his face grew pale and his smile faded. He looked at the doctor and asked in a trembling voice, "Will I start to die right away?"

In his innocence, the brother thought he had to give all of his blood in order to save his sister.

✥ Obstacle in Our Path ✥

A king had a boulder placed on a road. He hid to watch if anyone would remove the huge rock. Some of the king's wealthiest merchants and courtiers came by and simply walked around it. Many loudly blamed the king for not keeping the roads clear, but none did anything about removing the stone.

A peasant carrying a load of goods approached. He laid down his burden and tried to move the stone aside. After pushing and straining, he succeeded. When the peasant picked up his burden, he noticed a purse lying in the road where the boulder had been. It contained gold coins and a note from the king indicating the gold was for the person who removed the boulder.

The peasant learned what many of us never have:
Every obstacle presents an opportunity to improve our condition.

✞ Three Things in Life That . . . ✞

Once gone, never come back:

1. Time
2. Words
3. Opportunity

May never be lost:

1. Peace
2. Hope
3. Honesty

Are most valuable:

1. Love
2. Self-confidence
3. Friends

Are never certain:

1. Dreams
2. Success
3. Fortune

Make a man or woman:

1. Hard work
2. Sincerity
3. Commitment

Can destroy a man or woman:

1. Alcohol

2. Pride

3. Anger

Are truly constant:

1. Father

2. Son

3. Holy Ghost

♰ Dedicated to Michael Q ♰

My brother Michael thinks God lives under his bed. At least that is what I heard him say one night. He was praying aloud in his bedroom, and I stopped outside his door to listen. "Are you there, God?" he asked. "Where are you? Oh, I see You under the bed." I giggled softly and tiptoed to my room. Michael's unique perspectives are often a source of amusement. But that night something else lingered long after the humor.

I realized for the first time the very different world he lives in. He was born twenty years ago, mentally disabled as a result of a routine baby vaccination. Apart from his six-foot, two-inch stature he exhibits few traits of an adult. He reasons and communicates with the capacity of a seven-year-old, and always will. He will probably always believe that God lives under his bed, that Santa Claus is the one who fills the space under our tree at CHRISTmas, and that airplanes stay up in the sky because angels carry them.

I wondered if Michael realizes he is different. Is he ever dissatisfied with his monotonous life: up before dawn each day, off to a workshop for the disabled, home to walk our *bichon frisé,* return to a dinner of his favorite Cheerios and milk, and later to bed? The only variation is laundry, when he hovers excitedly over the washer and dryer like a mother with a newborn.

He does not seem dissatisfied. He lopes to the bus every morning at 7:05, eager for a day of simple work. He wrings his hands expectantly while water boils on the stove before dinner and stays up late twice a week to gather our dirty laundry for his next day's duty.

And Sundays; oh yes, the glory of Sundays. Dad drives Michael to the gas station to pick up donut holes and sit and watch cars pass through the car wash. They speculate animatedly about the occupation of the car owners. "That one's a fireman," Michael shouts and claps his hands. His anticipation is so keen he can hardly sleep on Saturday nights.

So goes his world of daily rituals and weekend field trips. He does not know what it means to be discontent. His life is simple. He will never know the entanglements of wealth or power, and he does not care what brand of clothing he wears or how many songs are on his i-Pod. His needs have always been met, and he does not fret that one day they may not be.

Michael is never so happy as when he is working. His hands are diligent. When he unloads the clothes dryer or washes the car, he is fully engaged. He does not shrink from a job and does not stop until it is finished. But when his tasks are done, he knows how to relax. He is not obsessed with his work.

His heart is pure. He believes everyone tells the truth, promises must be kept, and when you are wrong, you apologize, not argue. Free from pride, Michael is not afraid to cry when he is hurt, angry, or sorry. He is always transparent, always sincere.

He trusts God, is friends with Him in a manner that is tough for a mature person to accept. Not confined by intellectual reasoning, he approaches God as a child. God seems like his closest companion.

In moments of doubt and frustration with my Christianity, I envy the security Michael has in his uncomplicated faith. It is then I am willing to admit he possesses divine knowledge that rises above my mortal questions. It is then I realize he is not the one with a handicap. I am.

My obligations, my fear, my pride, my circumstances, my fallen humanity become disabilities when I fail to trust them to God's care. Who knows if Michael comprehends matters I can never learn? After all, he has spent his entire life in that state of innocence, praying after dark and soaking up the goodness and love of God.

One day, when the mysteries of heaven are revealed and we are stunned at how near our hearts God truly is, I will know God heard the prayers of a boy who believed that He lived under his bed.

Michael will not be surprised at all.

✟ Satan's Plan ✟

(If you are too busy to read, Satan's plan is working.)

Satan held a worldwide convention of demons. At the opening, he said, "We can't keep Christians from going to church, reading their Bibles, knowing the truth, or forming an intimate relationship with their Savior.

"Once they gain a connection with Jesus, our control over them is terminated. So, let them go to church, have covered dish dinners and bingo nights. But steal their time, so they don't have time to develop a real relationship with Him.

"This is what I want you to do," advised the devil. "Distract them throughout their day from maintaining that vital link with Jesus."

"How shall we do this?" his demons inquired.

He answered confidently, "Keep them busy in the nonessentials of life and invent innumerable schemes to occupy their empty minds:

> Tempt them to spend, spend, spend, and borrow, borrow, borrow.
>
> Persuade wives to go to work and husbands to work seven days a week, ten hours a day, so they can afford their empty lifestyles.
>
> Keep them from spending time with their children so families fragment and homes offer no escape from the pressures of work.
>
> Over-stimulate their minds so they cannot hear that 'still, small voice.'
>
> Entice them to play their radio or iPod when they drive and keep their TV, VCR, CDs, and PCs on in their homes constantly.
>
> Have every store and restaurant play non-biblical music to jam their minds and break their union with Christ.
>
> Fill coffee tables with magazines and papers.
>
> Pound their minds with twenty-four-hour news.
>
> Invade their driving with billboards.
>
> Flood their mailboxes with junk mail, sweepstakes, newsletters, and promotions offering free products, services, and false hopes.

Show beautiful models on magazines and TV, so husbands will believe that outward beauty is what's important. They'll become dissatisfied with their wives.

Give their wives headaches and keep them too tired to love their husbands. The husbands will look elsewhere.

Give them Santa to distract them from teaching children the real meaning of CHRISTmas.

Give them a bunny so they won't talk about His resurrection and power over sin and death.

Let them be excessive in recreation and exhaust themselves.

Keep them too busy to enjoy nature and reflect on God's creation. Send them to fun parks, sporting events, and movies instead.

Keep them busy so when they meet for spiritual fellowship, they will leave with troubled consciences.

Crowd their lives with so many causes they have no time to seek power from Jesus. Soon they will labor in their strength and sacrifice their health and family for the good of the cause."

"It will work, it will work," rejoiced the devil's disciples.

It was quite a fiendish plan. The demons easily executed their assignment, causing Christians to have little time for their God or families and no time to tell others about the power of Jesus to change lives.

*Busy stands for **B**eing **U**nder **S**atan's **Y**oke*

✞ 'Cause My Cup Has Overflowed ✞

I've never made a fortune, and it's probably too late now.
But I don't worry about that much, I'm happy anyhow.
And as I go along life's way, I'm reaping better than I sowed.
I'm drinking from my saucer, 'cause my cup has overflowed.

Haven't got a lot of riches, and sometimes the going's tough,
I've got loving ones around me, and that makes me rich enough.
I thank God for his blessings, and the mercies He's bestowed.
I'm drinking from my saucer, 'cause my cup has overflowed.

I remember times when things went awry and wore my faith thin;
Soon, the dark clouds broke and the sun peeped through again.
So Lord, help me not to gripe about the tough rows I have hoed.
I'm drinking from my saucer, 'cause my cup has overflowed.

If God gives me strength and courage when the way grows steep and rough,
I'll not ask for other blessings, I'm already blessed enough.
And may I never be too busy to help others bear their loads.
Then I'll keep drinking from my saucer, 'cause my cup has overflowed.

✟ Hospital Window ✟

Two seriously ill men occupied the same hospital room. One was required to sit in his bed each day for an hour to help drain fluid from his lungs. His bed was next to the lone window. The roommate had to spend all his time flat on his back.

The men talked for hours about their wives, families, homes, jobs, vacations, and much more. Every afternoon, the man by the window would sit up and offer his supine roommate a vivid description of what he saw. The bedridden man began to live for these periods when his world would be enlivened by the colorful activity of the world through the window.

The window overlooked a grassy park with a lovely lake. Ducks and swans played on the water while children sailed model boats. Young lovers strolled arm in arm amidst flowers of every hue and a fine view of the distant city skyline could be had. As the one narrated the exquisite details, the other would close his eyes and imagine the picturesque scene.

One warm afternoon, the man reported a passing parade. Although the other could not hear the band, he could see it in his mind's eye as his friend portrayed it in dramatic detail. Days and weeks passed in this delightful manner.

One morning, the nurse arrived for their baths and found the lifeless body of the man by the window. He had died peacefully in his sleep. Saddened, she called the attendants to remove the body.

When it seemed appropriate, the other man requested to be moved next to the window. The nurse was happy to make the switch. After making sure he was comfortable, she left. Slowly, painfully, he propped himself up on the windowsill to take his first peek at the world outside. He was astounded to see the blank wall of the building next door

The man called the nurse, "What compelled him to describe such wonderful sights."

She further astonished him, "I don't know. He was blind and didn't know the wall was there."

Shared grief is half the sorrow, but happiness when shared is doubled.

✝ You'll Find Jesus There ✝

"Tomorrow morning," the surgeon began, "I'll open your heart and—"

"You'll find Jesus there," the boy interrupted.

The surgeon glanced at the ceiling, annoyed, "I'll cut your heart open," he continued, "to see how much damage has been done—"

"But when you open my heart, you'll find Jesus there," insisted the boy.

The surgeon turned to the parents who sat quietly. "When I see how much damage has been done, I'll sew his heart and chest back up and decide what to do next."

"But you'll find Jesus in my heart. The Bible says He lives there. The hymns all say He lives there. You'll find Him in my heart."

The surgeon lost his temper, "I'll tell you what I'll find in your heart. I'll find damaged muscle, low blood supply, and weakened vessels. And I'll find out if I can make you well."

"You'll find Jesus there, too. He lives there," the boy persisted. The surgeon left in irritation.

After the operation, in his office the surgeon recorded his notes, "Damaged aorta and pulmonary vein with widespread muscle degeneration. No hope for transplant or cure. Therapy: painkillers and bed rest. Prognosis:" he paused, "death within a year."

He closed the recorder but had more to say. "Why?" he cried in anguish,

"Why did You do this? You've put him here. You've put him in this pain. You've cursed him to an early death. Why?"

The Lord answered, "The boy, My lamb, was not meant for your flock for long. He is part of My flock and will forever be. With Me, he will have no pain and will be comforted beyond your imagination. His parents will one day join him and they will know peace, too."

The surgeon's tears were hot, but his anger hotter. "You created that boy and You created that heart. He'll be dead in months. Why?"

The Lord replied, "The boy, My lamb, shall return to My flock, for he has done his duty: I did not place My lamb with your flock to lose him, but to retrieve another lost lamb."

The surgeon wept.

Later, the surgeon sat beside the boy's bed with the boy's parents across from him. The boy awoke and whispered, "Did you cut open my heart?"

"Yes," said the surgeon.

"What did you find?" asked the boy.

"I found Jesus there," said the surgeon.

✙ When Tomorrow Starts without Me ✙

When tomorrow starts without me and I'm not there to see
If the sun should rise and your eyes fill with tears for me,
I wish so much you wouldn't cry the way you did today
While thinking of the many things we didn't get to say.

I know how much you love me—as much as I love you.
Each time that you think of me, I know you'll miss me too.
But when tomorrow starts without me, please, try to understand
That an angel came and called my name and took me by the hand.

She said my place was ready in heaven far above.
And I'd have to leave behind all those I dearly love.
But as I turned to walk away, a tear fell from my eye.
For all my life, I'd always thought I didn't want to die.

I had so much to live for, so much left to do,
It seemed almost impossible that I was leaving you.
I thought of all the yesterdays, the good ones and the bad,
I thought of all we'd shared and all the fun we'd had.

If I could relive yesterday, just even for a while,
I'd say good-bye and kiss you and maybe see you smile.
But then I fully realized that this could never be,
For emptiness and memories would take the place of me.

When I thought of worldly things I might miss come tomorrow,
I thought of you and, when I did, my heart was filled with sorrow.
But when I walked through heaven's gates, I felt so much at home.
When God looked down and smiled at me from His golden throne.

He said, "This is eternity and all I've promised you.
Today your life on earth is past and here life starts anew.
I promise no tomorrow but today will always last,
And since each day's the same, there's no longing for the past.

You have been so faithful, so trusting, and so true.
Even though there were times you did some things you knew you
shouldn't do.
But you have been forgiven and now at last you're free.
So won't you come and take My hand and share My life with Me?"

So when tomorrow starts without me, don't think we're far apart,
For every time you think of me, I'm right here in your heart.

Origin of Health Maintenance Organizations

In the beginning, God covered the earth with broccoli, spinach, cauliflower, and colorful, tasty vegetables of all kinds so man and woman would live long and healthy lives.

Using God's bountiful gifts, Satan created Ben and Jerry's and Krispy Kreme. He added, "Do you want hot fudge with that?"

Man replied, "Yes," and woman responded, "I'll have another with sprinkles." Lo and behold, they gained ten pounds.

God created healthy yogurt that woman might keep the figure that man found so fair.

Satan brought forth white flour from the wheat, sugar from the cane, and combined them. Woman went from size two to ten.

God said, "Try my fresh green salad."

Satan presented crumbled bleu cheese dressing and garlic toast on the side. Man and woman unfastened their belts following the repast.

God said, "I have sent you heart-healthy vegetables and olive oil in which to cook them."

Satan brought forth deep-fried coconut shrimp, butter-dipped lobster chunks, and chicken fried steak so large it required its own platter. Man's cholesterol readings shot through the roof.

God brought forth running shoes so that his children might lose those extra pounds.

Satan came forth with cable TV and the remote control so man would not have to toil changing channels. Man and woman laughed and cried before the flickering light and began wearing stretch jogging suits.

God brought forth the potato, naturally low in fat and brimming with potassium and good nutrition.

Satan peeled off the healthy skin, sliced the starchy center into chips, deep-fried them in animal fats, and added copious quantities of salt. Man and woman put on more pounds.

God offered lean beef so that man might consume fewer calories and still satisfy his appetite.

Satan created McDonald's and the ninety-nine-cent double cheeseburger and suggested, "Do you want fries with that?" Man replied, "Yes, and can you super size 'em." Satan did and assessed, "It is good." Man went into cardiac arrest.

God sighed and created quadruple bypass surgery.

Satan craftily created HMOs.

⸸ Things Aren't Always What They Seem ⸸

Two traveling angels stopped to spend the night in the home of a wealthy family. The family was rude and refused to lodge the angels in the mansion's guest room. Instead, the angels were put up in a small space in the cold basement.

As they made their bed on the concrete floor, the older angel noticed a hole in the wall and repaired it. The younger angel asked why. He replied, "Things aren't always what they seem."

The next night, the pair came to rest at the house of a poor, but hospitable farmer and his wife. After sharing what little food they had, the couple let the angels have their bed to enjoy a comfortable night's sleep.

When the sun came up the next morning, the angels found the farmer and his wife in tears. Their only cow, whose milk had been their sole income, lay dead in the field.

The younger angel was infuriated and asked the older angel, "How could you have allowed this to happen? The first man had everything; yet, you helped him. The second family had little but was willing to share everything, and you let the cow die."

"Things aren't always what they seem," the older angel repeated. "When we stayed in the basement of the mansion, I saw gold stored in that hole in the wall. Since the owner was obsessed with greed and unwilling to share, I sealed the wall so he wouldn't find it.

"Last night as we slept in the farmer's bed, the angel of death came for his wife. I gave him the cow instead."

⸸ Now I've Said My ABCs ⸸

Although things are not perfect
Because of trial or pain
Continue in thanksgiving
Do not begin to blame.
Even when the times are hard
Fierce winds are bound to blow
God is forever able
Hold on to what you know.
Imagine life without His love

Joy would cease to be
Keep thanking Him for all the things
Love imparts to thee.
Move out of "Camp Complaining"
No weapon that is known
On earth can yield the power
Praise can do alone.
Quit looking at the future
Redeem the time at hand
Start every day with worship
To "thank" is a command.
Until we see Him coming
Victorious in the sky
We will run the race with gratitude
'**X**alting God most high
Yes, there will be good times and, yes, some will be bad, but
Zion waits in glory, where none are ever sad.

Now I've said my ABC's, tell me what you think of me.

✝ Lord, Teach America to Pray ✝

Lord, we would bow in need of Thee
Throughout this land from sea to sea,
From where Atlantic's breakers roar
To blue Pacific's golden shore.
Oh, may we all in longing say,
Lord, teach America to pray.

May we our sins to Thee confess,
Pleading in faith Thy righteousness,
May we again come to Thy throne,
Returning that which is Thine own.
Our broken hearts before Thee lay.
Lord, teach America to pray.

May our good land be true and just,
Her motto e'er "In God We Trust."
May she be guided by Thy Word,
Thy wisdom in her walls be heard.
May all who love her plead today,
Lord, teach America to pray.

And as her flag unfurls on high
Its starry splendor to the sky,
May we, in grateful thanks to Thee
Who gave to us this land so free,
Preserve her freedom in Thy way.
Lord, teach America to pray.

To pray that cruel wars may cease,
That to the world may come Thy peace,
That ever, always, at Thy feet
We may attain communion sweet.
In loving trust to Thee we say,
Lord, teach America to pray.

✟ In God We Trust ✟

A friend and her husband were invited to spend a weekend at the home of her husband's employer. My friend was nervous since the employer was very wealthy with a fine home on the water and cars that cost more than her house.

The first day and evening went well and she was delighted to have this rare glimpse into how the very well-off lived. Her husband's employer was generous as he hosted them at the finest restaurants. Knowing she would never have the opportunity to indulge in this extravagance again, she enjoyed herself freely.

About to enter an exclusive restaurant that evening, the boss was walking slightly ahead of her and her husband. He stopped abruptly and gazed down on the pavement for a silent moment.

She wondered if they were supposed to pass him. There was nothing on the ground except a single darkened penny and cigarette butts. The man picked up the penny, held it high, grinned, and placed it in his pocket as if it were a treasure.

How absurd. What need did this man have for a lone penny? Why would he take time to stop and pick it up?

Throughout dinner, the scene nagged her. She could stand it no longer and casually mentioned that her daughter had a coin collection and asked if the penny he found had been of value.

A smile crept across his face as he reached into his pocket for the penny and held it for her to see. She had seen many before. What was the point?

He said politely, "Read what it says."

She read the words, "United States of America."

"Read further," he asked.

"One cent?" she replied.

"Keep reading," he suggested.

"In God We Trust?" she responded.

"Yes," he sighed.

"And?" she inquired, perplexed.

"If I trust in God, the name of God is holy, even on a coin. Whenever I find one, I read that inscription. It is recorded on every U.S. coin but we do not seem to notice.

"God drops a message right in front of me encouraging me to trust Him. Who am I to pass it by? I stop and pray to discern if my trust is in God at that moment. I pick the coin up as a response to God; that I do trust in Him.

"For a short time, at least, I cherish it as if it were gold. I believe it is God's way of starting a conversation with me. Lucky for me, God is patient and pennies are plentiful."

✟ Pennies from Heaven ✟

I found a penny today just lying on the ground.
But it's not just any penny, this little coin I've found.
Found pennies come from heaven, that's what my Grandpa told me.
He said angels toss them down. Oh, how I loved the story.

He said when an angel misses you, they toss a penny down;
Sometimes to cheer you up, to make a smile out of your frown.
So, don't pass by that penny when you're feeling blue.
It may be a penny from heaven that an angel's tossed to you.

✝ Gift ✝

A young man prepared to graduate from college. For months, he admired a fancy sports car in a dealer showroom. Knowing his father could afford it, he told him that was what he wanted.

As graduation approached, the young man awaited signs that his father had purchased the car. On the day of graduation, his father called him to his private study to inform him how proud he was to have such a fine son. He told him how much he loved him and handed him an elegantly wrapped gift.

Curious and somewhat disappointed, the young man opened the gift to find a lovely, leather-bound Bible with his name embossed in gold. In an angry, raised voice, he protested, "With your money, all you give me is a Bible?" and stormed out of the house.

Many years passed. The young man was very successful in business, had a stylish home and wonderful family. He realized that his father was very old and thought he should repair relations since he had not seen him since graduation.

Before he could, he received a telegram informing him that his father had passed away and willed his possessions to him. He needed to come home immediately and take charge.

When he arrived, a wave of sadness and regret pierced his heart. He searched through his father's desk and found the Bible, wrapped as he had left it years ago. With teary eyes, he leafed through the pages to where His father had underlined a verse, Matthew 7:11. "If you, then, though you are evil, know how to give good gifts to your children, how much more will your Father in heaven give good gifts to those who ask him?"

As he read, a car key dropped from inside the Bible. It held a tag from the dealer who had the sports car he had desired. On the tag was the date of his graduation and the words "Paid in full."

✝ New School Prayer ✝

Now I sit me down in school
Where praying is against the rule.
For this great nation under God
Finds mention of Him very odd.

If Scripture now the class recites,
It violates the Bill of Rights.
And anytime my head I bow
Becomes a Federal matter now.

Our hair can be purple, orange, or green,
That's no offense; it's a freedom scene.
The law is specific, the law is precise.
Prayers spoken aloud are a serious vice.

For praying in a public hall
Might offend someone with no faith at all.
In silence alone we must meditate,
God's name is prohibited by the state.

We're allowed to cuss and dress like freaks,
And pierce our noses, tongues, and cheeks.
They've outlawed guns, but first the Bible.
To quote the good book makes me liable.

We can elect a pregnant senior queen,
And the "unwed daddy," our senior king.
It's inappropriate to teach right from wrong,
We're taught that such judgments do not belong.

We can get our condoms and birth controls,
Study witchcraft, vampires, and totem poles.
But the Ten Commandments are not allowed,
No word of God must reach this crowd.

It's scary here I must confess,
When chaos reigns the school's a mess.
So, Lord, this silent plea I make,
Should I be shot; my soul please take.

And You Expect Me Not to Pray

After being interviewed by school administrators, the teaching prospect summarized: "Let me see if I've got this right. You want me to go into a room full of kids and fill their every waking moment with a love for learning. I'm supposed to instill a sense of pride in their ethnicity, modify their disruptive behavior, observe them for signs of abuse, and censor their T-shirt messages and dress habits.

"You want me to wage a war on drugs and sexually-transmitted diseases, check their backpacks for weapons, and raise their self-esteem. You want me to teach them patriotism, good citizenship, sportsmanship, fair play, how to register to vote, how to balance a checkbook, and how to apply for a job.

"I'm to check their heads for lice, maintain a safe environment, recognize signs of antisocial behavior, and make sure that all students pass the mandatory state exams, even those who don't come to school regularly or complete any of their assignments.

"I'm to guarantee that the handicapped students receive an equal education regardless of the extent or nature of their disability.

"I'm to communicate regularly with the parents by letter, phone, newsletter, and report card.

I'm to accomplish this with a piece of chalk, a computer, a few books, a bulletin board, a big smile, and a salary that qualifies my family for food stamps.

"And, you expect me not to pray."

✟ Did Anyone Ever Tell You? ✟

Did anyone ever tell you just how special you are?
The light that you emit might even light a star.

Did anyone ever tell you how good you make others feel?
Somebody out here is smiling about love that is so real.

Did anyone ever tell you how often, when they were sad,
Your e-mail made them smile? In fact it made them glad.

For the time you spend e-mailing and sharing whatever you find
There are no words to thank you but somebody thinks you're fine.

✟ If I Were the Devil I Would . . . ✟

Gain control of the most powerful nation in the world.

Delude their citizens into thinking that their power had come from man's effort, instead of God's blessings.

Promote an attitude of loving things and using people, instead of the other way around.

Dupe entire states into promoting gambling for revenue.

Convince people that character is not an issue when it comes to leadership.

Make it legal to kill unborn babies.

Make it socially acceptable to take one's life and invent machines to make it convenient.

Cheapen human life as much as possible so that the lives of animals are valued more than humans.

Take God out of the schools where even the mention of His name is grounds for a lawsuit.

Produce drugs that sedate the mind and target the young by paying sports heroes to advertise them.

Control the media, so that each night's broadcast could pollute the mind of every family member with my agenda.

Attack the traditional family of mother, father, and children, the backbone of any nation.

Make divorce easy, even fashionable. If the family crumbles, so does the nation.

Compel people to express their most depraved fantasies on canvas and movie screens and call it art and freedom of speech.

Proclaim that some people are born homosexual and that their lifestyles should be accepted.

Have right and wrong determined by a few who call themselves authorities and refer to their agenda as politically correct.

Persuade people that the church is irrelevant and out of date and the Bible is for the naïve.

Dull the minds of Christians and have them believe that prayer is not important and faithfulness and obedience are optional.

If I were the devil, I would leave things pretty much the way they are and give myself a bonus for a job well done.

☦ Morning Blessing ☦

This morning when I awakened and saw the sun above,
I softly said, "Good morning, Lord, bless everyone I love."
Right away I thought of you and said a loving prayer,
That He would bless you specially to keep you free from care.

I thought of all the happiness a day could hold in store,
I wished it all for you because no one deserves it more.
I felt so warm and good inside, my heart was all aglow.
I know God heard my prayers for you, He hears them all, you know.

Spiritual Humor e-Soup — *A Compilation of Amusing Messages from the Internet*

Satan Goes to Church

Minutes before service, the townspeople were sitting in their pews and talking. Suddenly, Satan appeared at the front of the church. Everyone screamed and rushed for the front entrance, trampling each other in a frantic effort to get away from evil incarnate.

The church emptied except for an elderly gentleman who sat calmly in his pew, oblivious to God's ultimate enemy in his presence. Satan swaggered to the old man and said, "Don't you know who I am?"

The man replied, "Yep, sure do."

"Aren't you afraid of me?" Satan asked.

"Nope, sure ain't," said the man.

"Don't you realize I can kill you with a word?" threatened Satan.

"Don't doubt it for a second," returned the old man.

"Did you know I could cause you profound, horrifying agony for eternity?" persisted Satan.

"Yep," was the even reply.

"And you're still not afraid?" asked Satan.

"Nope," said the old man.

More than a little perturbed, Satan asked, "Why aren't you afraid of me?"

The man calmly replied, "Been married to your sister for forty-eight years."

✟ I Am Thanking You Now ✟

I am not going to wait until I see results or receive rewards. I am thanking You now.

I am not going to wait until I feel better or things look brighter. I am thanking You now.

I am not going to wait until people apologize or stop criticizing me. I am thanking You now.

I am not going to wait until the pain in my body fades. I am thanking You now.

I am not going to wait until my financial situation improves. I am thanking You now.
I am not going to wait until the children are asleep and the house quiet. I am thanking You now.
I am not going to wait until I get a promotion or the job. I am thanking You now.
I am not going to wait until the journey eases or the challenges subside. I am thanking You now.
I am thanking You now because of what You have already done.
I am thanking You now because I am alive.
I am thanking You now because I made it through the day's difficulties.
I am thanking You now because I have walked around the obstacles.
I am thanking You now because I have the opportunity to do more and better.
I am thanking You now because, Father, You have not given up on me.

✝ I Asked God ✝

I asked God for strength, that I might achieve;
I was made weak, that I might learn humbly to obey.

I asked God for health, that I might do greater things,
I was given infirmity, that I might do better things.

I asked God for riches, that I might be happy,
I was given poverty, that I might be wise.

I asked God for power, that I might have the praise of men,
I was given weakness, that I might feel the need of God.

I asked God for all things, that I might enjoy life,
I was given life, that I might enjoy all things.

I received nothing that I asked for but was given more than I could dream.
God granted not my wishes for wants but fully satisfied my needs.

♰ Gold Wrapping Paper ♰

A mother punished her five-year-old daughter for wasting a roll of expensive gold wrapping paper. Money was tight and she became upset when the child used the gold paper to decorate a box to place under the CHRISTmas tree. Nevertheless, the little girl brought the gift to her mother the next morning and said, "This is for you, Momma."

The mother was embarrassed by her earlier reaction, but her anger flared anew when she opened the box and found it empty. She spoke to her daughter harshly. "Don't you know when you give a present there's supposed to be a gift inside the package?"

The girl, with tears in her eyes, responded, "Momma, it's not empty. I blew kisses into it until it was full."

Christ's love is what you hear at CHRISTmas
when you take the time to stop opening gifts.

♰ Trouble Tree ♰

I hired a worker to help me restore an old farmhouse. He had a rough first day: A flat tire caused him to lose an hour of work, his electric drill died, and his ancient truck refused to start.

While I drove him home, he sat in stony silence. On arriving, he invited me to meet his family. As we walked up the stoop, he paused at a small tree and caressed the tips of the branches with both hands.

Entering his home, he underwent an amazing transformation. His tanned face was wreathed in a smile as he hugged his children and kissed his wife. At the dinner table, he glowed with love.

After dinner, we passed the tree on the way to my car and my curiosity got the better of me. "How come you touched that tree earlier?"

"That's my trouble tree," he said. "I know I can't avoid troubles on the job, but one thing's for sure, they don't belong in the home with my family. So, I hang 'em on the trouble tree every night and ask the Lord to take care of 'em. In the morning, I pick 'em back up.

"Funny thing, though," he said with a grin. "When I come out in the morning to pick 'em up, there aren't nearly as many as I remember hanging up the night before."

✟ Wooden Bowl ✟

A frail old man went to live with his son, daughter-in-law, and four-year-old grandson. The family ate together at the dinner table. But the elderly man's trembling hands and failing sight made eating difficult. Peas rolled off his spoon onto the floor and when he grasped the glass of milk, it spilled on the tablecloth.

The son and daughter-in-law became irritated. "We must do something about father," said the son. "I've had enough of his spilled milk, noisy eating, and food on the floor."

They set a small table in the corner. Grandfather ate alone while the others enjoyed dinner as a family. Since he had broken several dishes, his food was served in a wooden bowl.

When they glanced in his direction, they detected tears in his eye as he sat by himself. Yet, the only words the couple had for him were sharp admonitions when he dropped a fork or spilled food. The four-year-old witnessed everything in silence.

One evening before supper, the father noticed his son playing with wood scraps and asked the child sweetly, "What are you making, son?"

The boy responded, "I'm making a little bowl for you and mom to eat from when I grow up." The four-year-old smiled and went back to work.

The notion struck the parents speechless and tears streamed down their cheeks. Though no words were exchanged, they knew what must be done.

That evening the husband took his father's hand and lovingly guided him to the dinner table. For his remaining days, he ate every meal with the family. Neither husband nor wife seemed to care when a fork was dropped, milk spilled, or the tablecloth soiled.

Be nice to your children; one day they'll be choosing your nursing home.

✟ Jesus Checking In ✟

This is Jesus, passing through,
Thought that I might check on you.
Is your day going well, My friend?
I always have an ear to lend.

If you decide you need to talk,
Or side with me on a short walk;
I'll gladly take your hand in Mine
And listen to you for a time.

You see, I'm not so busy that
I can't take time to chat;
Or even lend a listening ear,
Because, you see, I'm always near.

I'll help to dry a tear or two;
I'll take away all fear from you.
I'll keep you warm when you are cold,
I'll comfort you when you grow old.

I'll cast the shadows from your day,
And give you sun to guide your way;
I'll lift you up when you are down,
A smile I'll give to cover your frown.

And when the day turns into night,
Your needn't fear, it'll be all right;
For I am just a prayer away,
Call on Me, I'll come and stay.

✟ Hello God ✟

I called tonight
To talk a little while.
I need a friend who'll listen
To my anxiety and trial.

You see, I can't quite make it
Through a day just on my own.
I need your love to guide me,
So I'll never feel alone.

I want to ask You please to keep
My family and friends safe and sound.
Come and fill their lives with confidence
For whatever fate they're bound.

Give me faith, dear God, to face
Each hour throughout the day,
And not to worry over things
I can't change in any way.

I thank You God for being home
And listening to my call,
For giving me such good advice
When I stumble and fall.

Your number, God, is the only one
That answers every time.
I never get a busy signal,
Never had to pay a dime.

So thank You, God, for listening
To my troubles and my sorrow.
Good night, God, I love You too,
And I'll call again tomorrow.

♱ The Bible in Fifty Words ♱

God made
Adam bit
Noah arked
Abraham split
Joseph ruled
Jacob fooled
Bush talked
Moses balked
Pharaoh plagued
People walked
Sea divided
Tablets guided
Promise landed
Saul freaked
David peeked
Prophets warned
Jesus born
God walked
Love talked
Anger crucified
Hope died
Love rose
Spirit flamed
Word spread
God remained

♱ We Need Someone Who Understands ♱

A farmer had four puppies he wanted to sell. To advertise, he painted a sign to nail to a post in his yard. As he was driving the final nail, a tug on his overalls caused him to look down into the eyes of a little boy.

"Mister," he said, "I'd like to buy one of your pups."

"Son," said the farmer, wiping sweat from his brow, "these puppies come from fine parents and cost a good deal of money."

Sad, the boy dropped his head, reached deep into his pocket, pulled out a handful of coins, and held them up to the farmer. "I've got thirty-nine cents. Is that enough to sneak a peek?"

"Sure," said the farmer, who let out a whistle and yelled, "Dolly." Dolly waddled out of the doghouse followed by four rambling balls of fur.

The boy stuck his head through the wood slats, eyes dancing in delight. As the dogs trotted toward him, he noticed a stir inside the doghouse. Another, noticeably smaller, fur ball appeared. This one awkwardly slid down the ramp and hobbled to catch up to the others.

The little boy pointed and exclaimed, "I want that tiny one."

The farmer knelt at the boy's side and said gently, "You don't want a runt that'll never be able to run and play with you like the others."

The little boy reached down and rolled up one leg of his trousers to reveal a steel brace running down both sides of his leg. Looking back at the farmer, he said, "Ya' see, sir, I don't run too well myself and he'll need someone who understands."

With tears in his eyes, the farmer picked up the pup and tenderly handed him to the little boy.

"How much?" asked the boy.

"No charge," answered the farmer. "There's no charge for love."

✟ God Gave Us Friends ✟

God knew that everyone needs companionship and cheer,
God knew that we need someone whose thoughts are always near.
He knew that we need someone kind to lend a helping hand,
Someone to gladly take the time to care and understand.

God knew that we all need someone to share each happy day,
To be a source of courage when troubles come our way.
Someone to be true to us whether near or far apart,
Someone whose love we'll always hold and treasure in our hearts.

✟ The Carpenter ✟

Two brothers on adjoining farms had their first serious rift in forty years of sharing machinery and trading labor and goods. What began as a minor misunderstanding exploded into an exchange of incendiary words followed by weeks of silence.

One morning, the older brother answered his door to find a man with a carpenter's toolbox. "I'm looking for a few days' work. Perhaps you have some jobs I could help with?"

The older brother said, "You bet. See the farm across the water? That's my neighbor; in fact, my younger brother. There was a lovely, grass-filled meadow between us until he bulldozed the river levee and separated us by this awful manmade creek.

"He did it to spite me but I plan to do him one better. I have a pile of lumber by the barn. I want you to build an eight-foot fence, so I can't see his place, his face, or his creek."

The carpenter replied, "I think I understand the situation. Give me nails and a posthole digger and I'll do a job that fills the need."

After helping gather the materials, the older brother left for town. The carpenter worked steadily measuring, sawing, and nailing. By sunset, when the farmer returned, he had completed construction.

The farmer's eyes gaped and jaw slacked. Instead of an obtrusive fence, there stood a bridge spanning the creek: a fine piece of carpentry appointed with handrails, light posts, and fluted abutments.

The neighbor, his younger brother, came running toward him with arms outstretched. "You are quite a fellow to build this bridge after what I've said and done."

The brothers raced from opposite ends of the bridge, met in the middle, and embraced with tears of remorse and shame staining their cheeks. They turned to see the carpenter hoist his toolbox onto his shoulder and walk off.

"No, wait. Stay a few days. I've a lot of other projects for you," pleaded the older brother.

The younger brother added, "Yes, I can use your help, too."

"I'd love to stay on," the carpenter said, "but I have more bridges to build."

✟ A Special Valentine ✟

—John 3:16

For God so lo**V**ed the world,
That He g**A**ve
His on**L**y
Begott**E**n
So**N**
Tha**T** whosever
Believeth **I**n Him
Should **N**ot perish,
But have **E**verlasting life.

✟ If I Knew ✟

If I knew it would be the last time
That I'd see you fall asleep,
I would tuck you in more tightly
And pray the Lord, your soul to keep.

If I knew it would be the last time
That I see you walk out the door,
I would give you a hug and kiss
And call you back for one more.

If I knew it would be the last time
I'd hear your voice lifted up in praise,
I would videotape each action and word,
So I could play them back day after day.

If I knew it would be the last time,
I could spare an extra minute
To stop and say, "I love you,"
Instead of assuming you would know I do.

If I knew it would be the last time
I would be there to share your day,
Well, I'm sure you'll have so many more,
So I can let just this one slip away.

For surely there's always tomorrow
To make up for an oversight,
And we always get a second chance
To make everything just right.

There will always be another day
To say, "I love you,"
And certainly there's another chance
To say our "Anything I can do?"

But just in case I might be wrong,
And today is all I get,
I'd like to say how much I love you
And I hope we never forget.

Tomorrow is not promised to anyone,
Young or old alike,
And today may be the last chance
You get to hold your loved one tight.

So if you're waiting for tomorrow,
Why not do it today?
For if tomorrow never comes,
You'll surely regret the day

That you didn't take that extra time
For a smile, a hug, or a kiss.
And you were too busy to grant someone
What turned out to be their one last wish.

So hold your loved ones close today,
And whisper in their ear,
Tell them how much you love them
And that you'll always hold them dear.

Take time to say, "I'm sorry,"
"Please forgive me," "Thank you," or "It's okay."
And if tomorrow never comes,
You'll have no regrets about today.

♱ ASAP ♱

There's work to do, deadlines to meet;
You've got no time to spare,
But as you hurry and scurry,
ASAP, Always Say a Prayer.

In the midst of family chaos,
Quality time is rare.
Do your best; let God do the rest.
ASAP, Always Say a Prayer.

It may seem like your worries
Are more than you can bear.
Slow down and take a breather,
ASAP, Always Say a Prayer.

God knows how stressful life is
He wants to ease our cares,
And He'll respond to all your needs.
ASAP, Always Say a Prayer.

✠ Red Fridays ✠

Increasingly, you will notice people wearing red on Fridays. Why? Americans who support our troops used to be called the silent majority. We are no longer silent and we are exhibiting our love for God and country in record-breaking numbers. We are not organized, overbearing, or boisterous. We receive no media coverage to reflect our message or our opinions.

We want to publicize that the vast majority of Americans support our troops. Our dignified and respectful show of support begins this Friday and continues until the troops come home. To send a deafening signal, every American who supports our men and women in uniform will wear something red. By word of mouth, e-mail, Internet, and other methods, let us spread the message and turn the United States into a sea of red every Friday.

If everyone who loves this country shares this e-mail with friends, family, acquaintances, neighbors, and co-workers, it will not be long before the country is attired in red. Our action will tell our soldiers that the once-silent majority is silent no more and on their side more than ever.

Spread the word and lead by example: Wear something red every Friday.

✠ What Lies on the Other Side ✠

Preparing to leave the examination room, the sick man admitted, "Doc, I'm afraid to die. What lies on the other side?"

Quietly, the doctor answered, "I don't know."

"You don't?" the man cried. "You, a Christian that doesn't know what's on the other side?"

From the other side of the door came scratching and whining. As the doctor opened the door, a dog sprang into the room and leaped on him with an eager display of affection.

The doctor said to the patient, "Did you notice my dog? He's never been in this room and didn't know what was waiting. He knew only that his master was on the other side. When the door opened, he rushed in without fear.

"I know little of death but I know one thing: my Master is on the other side and that's enough for me."

♱ God's Boxes

I have in my hands two boxes,
Which God gave me to hold.
He said, "Put all your sorrows in the black box,
And all your joys in the gold."

I heeded His words and in the two boxes
Both my joys and sorrows I stored.
But though the gold became heavier each day,
The black was as light as before.

With curiosity, I opened the black;
I wanted to find out why.
I saw, in the base of the box, a hole,
Which my sorrows had fallen out by.

I showed the hole to God and mused,
"I wonder where my sorrows could be."
He smiled a gentle smile and said,
"My child, they're all here with me."

I asked God why He gave me the boxes.
"Why the gold and the black with the hole?"
"My child, the gold is for you to count your blessings,
The black is for you to let go."

♱ How to Stay Young ♱

1. Try everything twice. A legendary epitaph: "Tried everything twice and loved it both times."
2. Keep only cheerful friends. The grouches pull you down. (Keep this in mind if you are one of those grouches.)

3. Keep learning about the computer, crafts, gardening, whatever. Never let the brain idle. "An idle mind is the devil's workshop." And the devil's name is Alzheimer.

4. Enjoy the simple things.

5. Laugh often, long, and loud, until you gasp for breath. If you have friends who make you laugh, spend lots of time with them.

6. The tears happen: endure, grieve, and move on. The only person who is with us our entire life is ourselves. Live while you are alive.

7. Surround yourself with what you love, whether it is family, pets, keepsakes, music, plants, or hobbies. Your home is your refuge.

8. Cherish your health. If it is good, preserve it; if it is unstable, improve it; if it is beyond what you can improve, get help.

9. Do not take guilt trips. Take a trip to the mall, even to the next county, to a foreign country, but not to where the guilt is.

10. Tell the people you love that you love them at every opportunity.

11. Today, forgive those who made you cry. You might not get a second chance.

✟ George Washington's Prayer for America ✟

Almighty God, we make our earnest prayer that Thou wilt keep the United States in Thy holy protection; that Thou wilt incline the hearts of the citizens to cultivate a spirit of subordination and obedience to government, and entertain a brotherly affection and love for one another and for their fellow citizens of the United States at large.

And finally that Thou wilt most graciously be pleased to dispose us all to do justice, to love mercy, and to demean ourselves with that charity, humility, and pacific temper of mind which were the characteristics of the Divine Author of our blessed religion, and without a humble imitation of whose example in these things we can never hope to be a happy nation.

Grant our supplication, we beseech Thee, through Jesus Christ our Lord. Amen.

♰ Expect the Unexpected ♰

The man whispered, "God, speak to me."
A meadowlark sang.
But the man did not hear.

The man yelled, "God, speak to me."
Thunder rolled across the sky.
But the man did not listen.

The man looked around and said, "God, let me see you."
A star shone brightly.
But the man did not see.

The man shouted, "God, show me a miracle."
A life was born.
But the man did not notice.

The man cried, "Touch me, God, and let me know you are here."
God reached down and touched the man.
But the man brushed the butterfly away and walked on.

The man entreated, "God, I need your help."
An e-mail arrived brimming with good news and encouragement.
But the man deleted it and continued in despair.

Do not miss a blessing because it is not packaged the way you expect.
Expect the unexpected; that is God at work.

There are no coincidences; only Godcidences.

✟ Dogs' Purpose ✟

As a veterinarian, I examined a ten-year-old Irish wolfhound named Belker. The owners, Ron, his wife, Lisa, and their little boy, Shane, were very attached to Belker and hoped for a miracle. Sadly, my exam revealed that Belker was dying of cancer.

I informed the family we could not do anything for him and offered to come to their home to put their pet to sleep. Ron and Lisa told me they thought it would be good for four-year-old Shane to observe and learn something from the experience.

The next day, I felt the familiar catch in my throat as Belker's family surrounded him. Belker seemed so calm; petting the old dog for the last time, I wondered if he understood what was going on.

Within a few minutes, Belker slipped away peacefully. The little boy seemed to accept Belker's transition without any difficulty or confusion. We sat together after Belker's death, bemoaning the fact that animal lives are shorter than human lives.

Shane, who had been listening quietly, piped up, "I know why."

Startled, we turned to him. What came out of his mouth stunned me. I had never heard a more comforting explanation.

"People are born so they can learn how to live a good life, like loving and being nice to everybody, right?" The four-year old continued, "Well, dogs already know how to do that, so they don't have to stay as long."

✟ Empty Egg ✟

Jeremy Forester was born with a twisted body and slow mind. At twelve years old, he was stuck in second grade, seemingly unable to learn. He exasperated his teacher, Doris Miller.

He would squirm in his seat, drool, and make grunting noises. At other times, he spoke clearly and distinctly, as if a spot of light had penetrated the darkness of his brain. However, he plain irritated his teacher.

She called his parents for a consultation. When the Foresters entered the empty classroom, Doris stated, "Jeremy belongs in a special school. It's not fair to him to be with younger children who don't have learning problems. There's a five-year gap between him and the others."

Mrs. Forester cried softly into a tissue while her husband spoke. "Miss

Miller, there is no school of that kind nearby. It would be a terrible shock for Jeremy if we had to take him out of this school. He likes it here."

After the meeting, Doris stared out the window at the snow in the schoolyard. The cold seemed to seep into her soul. She wanted to sympathize with the Foresters; after all, their only child had a terminal illness. However, it was not fair to keep him in her class; she had eighteen others to teach and Jeremy was a distraction.

He would never learn to read or write, so why waste more time. As she pondered, guilt washed over her. Here I am complaining when my problems are nothing compared to that family. Lord, help me be more patient with Jeremy. From that day, she tried to ignore his idiosyncrasies.

One day, dragging his limp leg, he approached her desk. "I love you, Miss Miller," he exclaimed loud enough for the class to hear.

The students snickered and Doris' face turned red. She stammered, "Wh—why that's very nice, Jeremy, please take your seat."

Spring sprung and the children became excited about the arrival of Easter. Doris related the Paschal story and to emphasize the idea of new life springing forth she gave each of the children a large plastic egg. "I want you to take this home and bring it back tomorrow with something inside that shows new life. Do you understand?"

"Yes, Miss Miller," the class, except for Jeremy, responded. He listened intently as his eyes never left her face. He did not even make his usual noises. Had he comprehended the meaning of Jesus' death and resurrection? Did he understand the assignment? She decided to call his parents and explain the project to them.

That evening, her kitchen sink stopped up and she waited an hour for the engineer to come and unclog it. After that, she shopped for groceries, ironed a blouse, prepared a math test, and completely forgot about Jeremy's parents.

The next day, the children came to class, talking excitedly as they placed their eggs in the wicker basket on her desk. After the math quiz, it was time to open the eggs.

In the first egg, Doris found a flower. "Oh, yes, a flower is surely a sign of new life. When plants peek through the ground, we know spring is here."

A small girl in the first row waved her arm and called out, "That's my egg, Miss Miller."

The second egg contained a plastic butterfly. Doris held it up, "We all know that a caterpillar changes and grows into a beautiful butterfly. Yes, that's new life, too."

Little Judy proudly announced, "Miss Miller, that one is mine."

The next egg held a rock with moss on it. Doris explained that moss, too, showed life.

Billy beamed from the back, "My daddy and I discovered that."

Doris opened the fourth egg and gasped: It was empty. *This must be Jeremy's*, she thought. *Of course, he didn't understand the lesson. If only I hadn't forgotten to phone his parents.* Because she did not want to embarrass him, she quietly set the egg aside and reached for another.

Suddenly, Jeremy shouted, "Miss Miller, aren't you going to talk about my egg?"

Flustered, Doris replied, "But Jeremy, your egg is empty."

He peered into her eyes and said softly, "Yes, but Jesus' tomb was empty, too." Time stopped.

When she could speak again, Doris asked, "Do you know why the tomb was empty?"

"Yes," Jeremy said, "Jesus was killed and put in there; then His Father raised Him up." The recess bell rang. While the children exuberantly ran out to the schoolyard, Doris cried. The cold inside her melted completely.

Three months later, Jeremy died. Those who paid their respects at the mortuary were surprised to see nineteen eggs decorating his casket: all of them empty.

Spiritual Humor e-Soup *A Compilation of Amusing Messages from the Internet*

Another Empty Egg

On Easter Sunday, the minister was preaching the children's sermon. He reached into his bag of props and pulled out an egg. He raised the egg and asked, "What's in here?"

"I know," exclaimed a little boy. "Pantyhose."

✣ I Cannot Change the Way I Am ✣

I cannot change the way I am,
I never really try,
God made me different and unique,
I never ask Him why.

If I appear peculiar,
There's nothing I can do,
You must accept me as I am,
As I've accepted you.

God made a casting of each life,
Then threw the old away,
Each child is different from the rest,
Unlike as night from day.

So often we will criticize
The things that others do,
But, do you know, they do not think
The same as me and you.

So God in all His wisdom,
Who knows us all by name,
Didn't want us to be bored,
That's why we're not the same.

✣ Love Will Find Its Way ✣

In Bethlehem a manger waits
Long ago—and so today
Where hatred-weary people pray
Love will come and lie there.

And so do countless stables stand
In hearts as harsh as desert lands
Rough shelters in the wind and sand
Love will come and stay there.

Love that opens fists of hate
Heaps up gold on beggars' plates
Love that shows a kindly face
To enemies and strangers.

And the walls of stables tremble so
When the winds of fear and judgment blow
For a stable hopes in love alone
And knows that love's the answer.

O Love, the prophet's only word
The only lesson left to learn
The only end of heaven's work
And the only road that goes there.

Love that sees with mercy's eyes
Holds its arms out open wide
Threads its loom with separate lives
And weaves them all together.

May the lamps of stables glow
Brightly that their light may go
For miles in the darkness so
Love will find its way there.

✝ How Much a Prayer Weighs ✝

Louise Redden, poorly dressed with the aura of defeat about her, entered a grocery store. She approached the owner and humbly asked if she could charge a few groceries. She explained that her husband was ill and unable to work; they had seven children and needed food.

The grocer scoffed and insisted she leave at once. Visualizing the family needs, she pleaded, "Please, sir. I'll bring you the money as soon as I can." He told her he could not give her credit since she did not have a charge account at his store.

A customer overheard the conversation and assured the grocer he would stand good for whatever she needed for her family.

The grocer in a reluctant tone inquired of Louise, "Do you have a list?"

Louise replied, "Yes sir."

"Put your grocery list on the scales and whatever the list weighs, I will give you that amount in groceries," he taunted.

Louise reached into her purse, took out a piece of paper, and scribbled on it. She carefully laid it on the scale with her head bowed. The grocer and the customer were astonished when the scale tipped to the bottom and stayed there.

The grocer turned to the customer and stated begrudgingly, "I can't believe it." The customer grinned as the grocer placed groceries on the opposing scale. The scale did not balance so he continued to pile groceries until the scale could hold no more.

Disturbed, the grocer grabbed the paper from the scale and received a greater shock. It was not a grocery list, but a prayer, "Dear Lord, you know my needs and I leave this in your hands."

He handed her the groceries in stunned silence. Louise thanked him and left. The customer handed a fifty-dollar bill to the grocer and said, "It was worth every penny. Only God knows how much a prayer weighs."

✟ I Am Home ✟

I am home in Heaven, dear ones.
Oh, so happy and so bright
There is perfect joy and beauty
In this everlasting light.

All the pain and grief is over,
Every restless tossing passed;
I am now at peace forever,
Safely home in Heaven at last.

Did you wonder I so calmly
Trod the valley of the shade?
Oh but Jesus' love illumined
Every dark and fearful glade.

And He came Himself to meet me
In that way so hard to tread;
And with Jesus' arm to lean on,
Could I have one doubt or dread?

Then you must not grieve so sorely,
For I love you dearly still.
Try to look beyond earth's shadows,
Pray to trust our Father's will.

There is work still waiting for you,
So you must not idly stand;
Do it now, while life remaineth
You shall rest in Jesus' land.

When that work is all completed,
He will gently call you Home;
Oh, the rapture of that meeting,
Oh, the joy to see you come.

✟ Your Angel's Name ✟

A baby asked God, "I understand you're sending me to earth tomorrow. How am I going to live there, being so small and helpless?"

God said, "Your angel will be waiting to take care of you."

The infant inquired further, "But tell me, here in heaven I don't have to do anything but sing, smile, and be happy."

God said, "Your angel will sing and smile for you. You will feel your angel's love and be very happy."

Again the child probed, "How am I going to be able to understand when people talk to me, if I don't know the language?"

God said, "Your angel will tell you the most beautiful and sweet words you will ever hear, and with patience and care, your angel will teach you how to speak."

"What am I to do when I want to talk to you?" the child countered.

God said, "Your angel will place your hands together and teach you how to talk to me."

"Who will protect me?" the child queried.

God said, "Your angel will defend you even if it means risking their life."

The child persisted, "I will always be sad because I will not see you anymore."

God said, "Your angel will talk to you about Me and show you the way back to Me."

In that instant, there was peace in Heaven but voices from Earth could be heard and the child hurriedly asked, "God, if I am to leave, please, tell me my angel's name."

God breathed, "Mom."

✟ The Lord's Baseball Game ✟

Freddy stood with the Lord to observe a baseball game between the Lord's team and Satan's team. The Lord's team was at bat in the bottom of the ninth, score tied 0 - 0 with two outs.

A batter named Love stepped to the plate and lined the first pitch for a single because "Love never fails."

The next batter named Faith also hit a single because "Faith works with Love."

The next was named Godly Wisdom. Satan wound up and threw his first pitch. Godly Wisdom looked it over and let it pass: ball one. Three more pitches and Godly Wisdom walked because he never falls for Satan's pitch.

The bases were loaded and the Lord turned to Freddy and told him He was going to bring in His star player. Up to the plate stepped Grace. Freddy observed, "He doesn't look like much." Satan's team relaxed when they saw Grace.

Satan wound up and fired his first pitch. To everyone's surprise, Grace hit the ball harder than anyone had ever seen. But Satan was not worried; his center fielder let very few get by. He leaped for the ball but it went right through his glove, hit him on the head, and sent him crashing to the ground. The crowds went wild as the ball bounded over the fence for a home run.

The Lord's team won and He asked, "Freddy, do you know why Love, Faith, and Godly Wisdom could get on base but could not win the game?"

Freddy answered, "No, Lord, I do not know."

The Lord explained, "If your love, faith, and wisdom had won the game, you would think you had done it by yourself. Love, Faith, and Wisdom will get you on base but only My Grace can get you home."

"For by Grace are you saved, it is a gift of God; not of works, lest any man should boast."

—Ephesians 2:8

✝ Five Finger Prayer ✝

Your thumb is nearest you. Begin by praying for those closest to you. They are the easiest to remember. To pray for our loved ones is a sweet duty.

The next finger is the pointing finger. Pray for those who teach, instruct, and heal: teachers, doctors, and ministers. They need support and wisdom in pointing others in the right direction.

Next, the tallest finger reminds us of our leaders. Pray for the president, leaders in business and government. They shape our nation and guide public opinion and need God's guidance.

The fourth, our ring finger, is our weakest, as any piano teacher will attest. It should remind us to pray for those who are weak, in trouble, or in pain. You cannot pray too much for them.

Lastly, our little finger, the smallest, indicates where we should place ourselves in relation to God and others. The Bible says, "The least shall be the greatest among you." Your pinkie should remind you to pray for yourself. By the time you have prayed for the others, your needs will be put into perspective and you will be apt to pray for yourself more appropriately.

✟ TV versus the Bible ✟

They lie on the table side by side
The Holy Bible and the TV guide.
One is well worn and cherished with pride.
Not the Bible, but the TV guide.
One is used daily to help folks decide.
No, not the Bible, but the TV guide.

As the pages are turned, what shall they see?
Oh, what does it matter, turn on the TV.
Then confusion reigns, they can't all agree
On what they should watch on the old TV.
So they open the book in which they confide,
No, not the Bible, but the TV guide.

The Word of God is seldom read,
Maybe a verse as they fall into bed.
Exhausted and sleepy and tired as can be;
Not from reading the Bible, from watching TV.

So then back to the table, side by side
Lie the Holy Bible and the TV guide.
No time for prayer, no time for the Word,
The plan of salvation is seldom heard.
But forgiveness of sin, so full and free,
Is found in the Bible, not on TV.

✞ Cell Phones versus the Bible ✞

The cell phone:

We carry it around in our purses or pockets.

We turn back to go get it if we forgot it.

We flip through it several times a day.

We use it to receive messages from the text.

We treat it like we could not live without it.

We give it to kids as a gift.

We use it as we travel.

We use it as a daily part of our lives and in emergencies.

We upgrade it to get the best version.

The Bible:

There are no additional charges for going over our minutes because He is eternal.

There is an exclusive plan for every human being because He knows every hair on our head.

There are no dropped calls because He never abandons us.

There are no roaming charges because He is available anywhere.

There are never any busy signals because He is available anytime.

There are no phone number changes because He is constant.

There is no battery to run out of power because He is all powerful.

There is no need to worry about service being disconnected because Jesus paid in advance.

Where have you placed *your* cell phone in your life? Your Bible? What might happen in your life if you valued your Bible as you value your cell phone?

✟ God Said, "No." ✟

I asked God to take away my habit.
God said, "No."
"It is not for me to take away, but for you to give it up."

I asked God to make my handicapped child whole.
God said, "No."
"His spirit is whole, his body is only temporary."

I asked God to grant me patience.
God said, "No."
"Patience is a byproduct of tribulation; it isn't granted, it must be earned."

I asked God to give me happiness.
God said, "No."
"I give you blessings; happiness is up to you.

I asked God to spare me pain.
God said, "No."
"Suffering draws you apart from worldly cares and brings you closer to me."

I asked God to make my spirit grow.
God said, "No."
"You must grow on your own, but I will prune you to make you fruitful."

I asked God for all things, that I might enjoy life.
God said, "No."
"I will give you life, so that you may enjoy all things."

I asked God to help me love others as much as He loves me.
God sighed, "Ah, finally you have the idea."
God said, "Yes."

✟ Ten Things God Won't Ask on That Day ✟

1. What model car you drove. He will ask how many people you drove who did not have transportation.

2. The square footage of your house. He will ask how many people you welcomed into your home.

3. About the clothes you had in your closet. He will ask how many you helped to clothe.

4. What your highest salary was. He will ask if you compromised your character to obtain it.

5. What your job title was. He will ask if you performed your job to the best of your ability.

6. How many friends you had. He will ask how many people to whom you were a friend.

7. In what neighborhood you lived. He will ask how you treated your neighbors.

8. About the color of your skin. He will ask about the content of your character.

9. Why it took you so long to seek salvation. He will take you to your mansion in heaven and not to the gates of hell.

10. How many people you evangelized with this message. He already knows your decision.

✟ Dad's Empty Chair ✟

A man's daughter asked the minister to come and pray with her father. When the minister arrived, he found the man lying in bed with his head propped on two pillows. An empty chair sat beside his bed. The minister assumed that the old fellow had been informed of his visit. "I guess you were expecting me," he said.

"No, who are you?" said the father.

The minister told him his name and remarked, "I saw the empty chair and figured you knew I was going to visit."

"Oh, the chair," said the bedridden man. "Would you mind closing the door?" he requested. Puzzled, the minister shut the door.

"I've never told anyone this, not even my daughter," explained the man. "I've never known how to pray. At church, I heard sermons about prayer, but it went over my head. So I abandoned any attempt at prayer until my best friend enlightened me, 'Johnny, prayer is a simply having a conversation with Jesus. Here's what I suggest. Sit in a chair; place an empty chair facing you, and, in faith, see Jesus seated on the chair. He promised, "I will be with you always." Speak to him like you're doing with me.'

"I tried it and liked it so much I do it a couple of hours every day. I'm careful though. If my daughter saw me talking to an empty chair, she'd either have a nervous breakdown or send me to the funny farm."

The minister was deeply moved by the story and encouraged him to continue on the journey. He prayed with him, anointed him with oil, and returned to the church.

Two nights later, the daughter called to inform the minister that her dad had died that day. "Did he die in peace?" he asked.

"Yes, when I was leaving, he called me to his bedside, said he loved me, and kissed me on the cheek. When I returned from the grocery store, I found him dead."

She added, "But there was something odd about his death. Apparently, before he died, he leaned over and rested his head on the chair beside the bed. What do you make of that?"

The minister wiped a tear from his eye and said, "I wish everybody could go like that."

✦ He Will Cover You with His Feathers and under His Wings You Will Find Refuge ✦

—Psalm 91:4

After a fire, forest rangers began their trek up a mountain to assess the inferno's damage. A ranger discovered a bird, petrified in ashes, perched statuesquely at the base of a tree.

Saddened by the ghostly sight, he tipped the bird over with a stick. When he did, three tiny chicks scurried from under their dead mother's wings. The loving mother, keenly aware of the impending disaster, had carried her offspring to the base of the tree. She gathered them under her wings, instinctively knowing that the toxic smoke would rise.

She could have flown to safety but had refused to abandon her babies. When the blaze arrived, the heat scorched her small body. But the mother remained steadfast. She had been willing to die, so those little ones under the cover of her wings would live.

✟ Presence of Jesus at CHRISTmas ✟

If you look for Me at CHRISTmas, you won't need a special star.
I'm no longer only in Bethlehem, I'm right there where you are.
You may not be aware of Me amid the celebrations.
You'll have to look beyond the stores and all the decorations.

But if you take a moment from your list of things to do
And listen to your heart, you'll find I'm waiting there for you.
You're the one I want to be with, you're the reason that I came,
And you'll find Me in the stillness as I'm whispering your name.

✟ How Do You Make People Feel? ✟

When I arrived at 2:30 A.M., the building was dark except for a dim light in a ground floor window. Under these circumstances, many drivers would merely honk, wait a minute, and drive away. But I had witnessed too many impoverished people who relied on taxis as their sole means of transportation. Unless a situation smelled of danger, I would go to the door, as the passenger might need assistance, I reasoned.

I walked to the door and knocked. "Wait a minute," answered a frail, elderly voice. I heard something being dragged across the floor. After a long pause, the door cracked open. A small woman in her eighties stood before me wearing a print dress and pillbox hat with a veil pinned on, like a starlet out of a 1940s movie.

By her side was a petite nylon suitcase. The apartment appeared as if no one had lived there for years: furniture covered by sheets, no clocks on the walls, no knickknacks or utensils on the counters, and a cardboard box filled with photos and glassware in the corner.

"Would you be so kind, as to carry my bag to the car?" she requested. I took the suitcase to the cab and returned to assist her. She took my arm and we walked slowly toward the curb. She kept thanking me for my kindness.

"It's nothing," I said, comforting her. "I treat my passengers the way I'd want my mother treated."

"Oh, you're such a good boy," she complimented.

When we settled in the cab, she gave me an address and asked, "Could you drive through downtown, please?"

"It's not the shortest way," I answered helpfully.

"Oh, I don't mind," she responded. "I'm in no hurry. I'm on my way to a hospice." I glanced in the rear-view mirror. Her eyes glistened. "I don't have any family left," she continued, "and the doctor says I don't have very long."

I furtively reached over, shut off the meter, and queried "What route would you like me to take?" For the next two hours, we toured the city.

She pointed out the building where she had worked as an elevator operator. We drove through the neighborhood where she and her husband had lived as newlyweds. She had me stop in front of a furniture warehouse that had been a ballroom where she had gone dancing as a girl. On occasion, she would ask me to pass slowly in front of a particular building or corner and she would silently stare into the darkness.

As the first glint of sun creased the horizon, she said, "I'm tired, let's go." We continued in silence to the address she had supplied.

The building looked like a small convalescent home with a driveway passing under a portico. Two orderlies approached as we pulled up. They must have been expecting her. They were solicitous and intent, watching her every move.

I opened the trunk and carried the small suitcase to the porch. The woman was seated in a wheelchair. "How much do I owe you?" she inquired, reaching into her purse.

"Nothing," I said.

"You have to make a living," she offered.

"There are other passengers," I responded.

Without thinking, I bent and hugged her. She held onto me tightly. "You gave an old woman a little moment of joy," she said. "Thank you."

I squeezed her warm, wrinkled hand and ambled into the morning light. Behind me a door shut softly: the sound of a life closing.

I did not pick up any passengers that shift and drove aimlessly, lost in thought: What if that sweet woman had gotten an angry driver or one who was impatient to end his shift? What if I had refused to take the run or had honked once and driven away? For the rest of that day, I could hardly speak.

On review, I do not think I have done anything more important in my life. We are conditioned to think that our lives revolve around great moments. But great moments often catch us unaware, beautifully wrapped in what most would consider a small one.

✟ 'Twas the Night Jesus Came ✟

'Twas the night Jesus came and all through the house,
not a person was praying, not one in the house.
The Bible was left on the shelf without care,
for no one thought Jesus would come there.

The children were dressing to crawl into bed,
not once ever kneeling or bowing their head.
And Mom in the rocking chair with babe on her lap
was watching the "Late Show" as I took a nap.

When out of the east there rose such a clatter,
I sprang to my feet to see what was the matter.
Away to the window I flew like a flash,
tore open the shutters, and lifted the sash.

When what to my wondering eyes should appear,
but angels proclaiming that Jesus was here.
The light of His face made me cover my head—
was Jesus returning just like He'd said?

And though I possessed worldly wisdom and wealth,
I cried when I saw Him in spite of myself.
In the Book of Life which He held in His hand
was written the name of every saved man.

He spoke not a word as He searched for my name;
when He said, "It's not here," my head hung in shame.
The people whose names had been written with love
He gathered to take to His Father above.

With those who were ready He rose without sound,
while all of the others were left standing around.
I fell to my knees but it was too late,
I'd waited too long and thus sealed my fate.

I stood and I cried as they rose out of sight,
Oh, if only I'd known that this was the night.
In the words of this poem the meaning is clear;
the coming of Jesus is now drawing near.

There's only one life and when comes the call,
We'll discover the Bible was true after all.

✝ A CHRISTmas Carol ✝

'Twas December twenty-fourth and all through the town
Not a sign of Baby Jesus was anywhere to be found.
The people were all busy with holiday-time chores
Like decorating, and baking, and shopping in stores.

No one sang, "Away in a manger, no crib for a bed."
Instead, they sang of Santa dressed up in bright red.
Mama watched TV, Papa drank beer from a tap,
As hour upon hour the presents they'd wrap.

When what from TV pierced both of their ears?
'Cept an ad which blared of a big sale at Sears.
So away to the mall they all flew like a flash
Buying things on credit 'cause nobody takes cash.

As they made their way home from their trip to the mall,
Did they think about Jesus? Heck no, not at all.
Their lives were so busy with holiday-time things
No time to remember Christ Jesus, the King.

There were presents to wrap and cookies to bake.
Left no time to remember Who died for their sake.
To pray to the Savior they had no time to stop.
They needed the time to shop till they dropped.

On Wal-mart, on Kmart, on Target, on Penney's,
On Hallmark, on Zales, a quick lunch at Denny's.
And up on the roof, there arose such a clatter
As Grandpa hung lights up on his new ladder.

He hung lights that would flash and lights that would twirl.
Yet, he never once prayed to Jesus, the Light of the World.
Forgotten was the Savior, no celebration for Him.
No remembrance of Jesus, no carol or hymn.

But forgiveness is freely given by God's only Son.
He understands our humanity and sins we have done.
Christ's eyes, how they twinkle. Christ's Spirit, how merry.
Christ's love so enormous, all our burdens He'll carry.

Instead of dreaming about all our presents and their worth
Let's put Christ back in CHRISTmas and rejoice in His birth.
On every occasion where "Christmas" appears in print
Won't you capitalize CHRIST as a not-so-subtle hint?

✝ Putting Christ Back into CHRISTmas Campaign ✝

The Spiritual e-Soup Ministry has inaugurated a campaign to put Christ back into CHRISTmas. The first initiative is a revision of the poem above, "A CHRISTmas Carol." Go to the website www.e-soupministry.com to learn more about how you can participate in the campaign.

✝ Life's Scars ✝

On a hot summer day, a little boy decided to go for a dip in the swimming hole behind his house. In a hurry, he ran out the back door, dropping behind shoes, socks, and shirt. He dove in without realizing that an alligator was weaving toward the shore.

In the house, his mother, peering out the kitchen window, saw the alligator moving closer and closer. In utter fear, she ran toward the water, yelling frantically. Her voice alarmed the little boy and he turned to swim to his mother.

From the dock, the mother grabbed her son by the arms as the gator snatched his legs. An incredible tug-of-war ensued: the alligator much stronger than the mother, but the mother too impassioned to let go. A farmer heard her screams and raced over and shot the alligator.

Remarkably, after weeks in the hospital, the little boy survived. His legs were terribly scarred by the vicious attack. On his arms were deep scratches where his mother's fingernails dug into his flesh in her effort to hang on to the son she loved.

A newspaper reporter interviewed the boy and asked if he could see his scars. The boy lifted his pant legs and, with obvious pride, said, "But look at the great scars on my arms, too. I have them because my mom wouldn't let go."

You and I can identify with that little boy. We have scars, too; not from an alligator, but from a painful past. Some are unsightly and have caused us deep regret. But, some are because God has refused to let go. In the midst of your struggle, He has been holding on for your life.

Scripture teaches: God loves you, you are a child of God, He wants to protect you and provide for you in every way. But, at times, we foolishly wade into dangerous situations, not knowing what lies ahead.

The swimming hole of life is filled with peril and we forget that evil is lurking. That is when the tug-of-war begins. If you have the scars of His love on your arms, be very grateful. He will never let you go.

✝ Dart Test ✝

Sally entered her seminary class and knew they were in for fun: A large target hung on the wall and darts lay on a table. Her teacher, Dr. Smith, was known for his elaborate object lessons.

When class began, he asked the students to draw a picture of a person they disliked and he would let them throw darts at the image. Sally's friend drew a girl who had stolen her boyfriend. Another drew his little brother. Sally drew a former friend and savored coloring garish pimples on the face.

The students eagerly lined up to throw darts. Some threw with such force that they ripped their target. Excitedly awaiting her turn, Sally was disappointed when Dr. Smith asked the class to return to their seats.

As she fumed about her missed chance to throw darts at her target, Dr. Smith peeled the large target from the wall to reveal a picture of Jesus. A hush enveloped the room as the students viewed the mangled image: Jagged marks covered His face and pierced His eyes.

Dr. Smith uttered, "In as much as ye have done it unto the least of these my brethren, ye have done it unto Me." (Matthew 25:40) Tears poured from their eyes as they focused on Christ's disfigured face and realized what they had done.

✝ If Only They Could Speak ✝

Beloved brethren, please hear us out. The Constitution, which proclaimed to the world in 1776 that all men were created equal by God with a God-given right to life, has recently granted all mothers an inviolable right to take our lives at their whim any time before birth.

In 1973, seven honorable but misguided justices so ruled, in spite of the fact that no such right exists in this document. Thirty-three years and forty-seven million homicides later, too many of our out-of-womb fellow citizens sit by as tacit sanctifiers of this slaughter of our innocent lives.

Beloved living, we await you on the other side for an explanation of why we had to die so you could live as you chose, unfettered by our apparently annoying existence. How did you allow "the cradle of life" to become "Death Row" for so many of us? Frankly, we do not understand why our brothers and sisters are still dying at the rate of three thousand per day as we speak.

Yet you, who call yourselves by His name and profess belief in the very God and His laws as did your founders, cannot unite on this critical issue, even when such unity unquestionably would have ended our holocaust long ago. This erosion of your constitutional, God-inspired heritage has cost us our lives. Reclaim the heritage or lose it. You cannot continue as you are.

We beg you to think about it, pray about it, and for the love of God and humanity, do something about it. You are all we have.

Signed, the least of His brethren

✠ I Pray That Your Prayers Be Answered ✠

A voyaging ship was wrecked during a storm and only two men made it to the safety of a small, desert island. Not knowing what to do, the survivors agreed they had no choice but to pray to God. However, to determine whose prayer was more worthy, they agreed to split up and stay on opposite sides of the island.

The first prayer was for food. In the morning, the first man discovered a fruit-bearing tree on his side of the land and ate from it. The other man's parcel of land remained barren.

After a week, the first man was lonely and decided to pray for a wife. The next day, a woman swam to his side of the land. On the other side of the island, there was nothing.

Soon, the first man prayed for a house, clothes, and more food. The next day, like magic, his wishes were granted. However, the second man had nothing.

Finally, the first man prayed for a ship, so he and his wife could escape the island. At sunup, a ship docked on his side of the island. He boarded with his wife and decided to leave the second man on the island. He considered him unworthy to receive God's blessings, since none of his prayers had been answered.

As the ship was about to depart, the first man heard a small, still voice, "Why are you abandoning your companion?"

"My blessings are mine alone, since I was the one who prayed for them," the man answered. "His prayers went unanswered, so he does not deserve anything."

"You are mistaken," the voice rebuked. "He had only one prayer, which I answered. If not for that, you would not have received any of my blessings."

"Tell me," the first man demanded, "what did he pray for that I should owe him anything?"

"He prayed that all your prayers be answered."

✝ Parable of the Spoons ✝

A holy man was holding a conversation with the Lord. "I would like to know what Heaven and Hell are like." The Lord led the holy man to two doors. He opened one of the doors and the holy man peered in. In the middle of the room was a large round table. In the middle of the table was a large pot of stew that smelled delicious and made the holy man's mouth water.

The people sitting around the table were thin and sickly; surprisingly, famished. They held spoons with long handles which made it possible to reach the pot of stew and withdraw a spoonful. But because the handle was longer than their arms they could not maneuver the spoons into their mouths.

The holy man shuddered at the sight of their misery and suffering. The Lord said, "You have seen Hell."

They opened the door to the next room which was exactly as the first: the large round table with the large pot of stew that made the holy man's mouth water. The people were equipped with the same long-handled spoons, but they were well nourished and plump, happy, and talking.

The holy man declared, "I don't understand."

"It is simple," responded the Lord, "it requires but one skill. You see, they have learned to serve one another while the greedy serve only themselves."

✟ Garden of Daily Living ✟

Plant three rows of peas:

1. Peas of mind
2. Peas of heart
3. Peas of soul

Plant four rows of squash:

1. Squash gossip
2. Squash indifference
3. Squash grumbling
4. Squash selfishness

Plant four rows of lettuce:

1. Lettuce be faithful
2. Lettuce be kind
3. Lettuce be patient
4. Lettuce really love one another

No garden is complete without turnips:

1. Turnip for meetings
2. Turnip for service
3. Turnip to help one another

To complete our garden, we must have thyme:

1. Thyme for each other
2. Thyme for family
3. Thyme for friends

Water with patience, cultivate with love, and reap what you sow.

⸸ I Like the Old Paths ⸸

When moms were at home and dads were at work. Brothers went into the army and sisters got married before having children.

Crime did not pay but hard work did and people knew the difference.

Moms could cook, dads would work, and children would behave.

Husbands were loving, wives were supportive, and children were polite.

Women wore the jewelry, men wore the pants.

Women looked like ladies, men looked like gentlemen, and children looked decent.

People loved the truth and hated a lie and they came to church to get in, not get out.

Hymns sounded Godly, sermons sounded helpful, rejoicing sounded normal, and crying sounded sincere.

Cursing was wicked, drinking was evil, and divorce was unthinkable.

The flag was honored, America was beautiful, and God was welcome.

We read the Bible in public, prayed in school, and preached from house to house.

To be called an American was worth dying for, to be called a Christian was worth living for, and to be considered a traitor was a shame.

Sex was a personal word, homosexual was an unheard word, and abortion was an illegal word.

Preachers preached because they had a message and Christians rejoiced because they had the victory.

Preachers preached from the Bible, singers sang from the heart, and sinners turned to the Lord to be saved.

A new birth meant a new life, salvation meant a changed life, and following Christ led to eternal life.

Being a preacher meant you proclaimed the Word of God, being a deacon meant you would serve the Lord, being a Christian meant you would live for Jesus, and being a sinner meant someone was praying for you.

Laws were based on the Bible, homes read the Bible, and churches taught the Bible.

Preachers were more interested in new converts than new clothes and new cars.

God was worshiped, Christ was exalted, and the Holy Spirit was respected.

Church was where you found Christians on the Lord's Day rather than on the creek bank, the golf course, or somewhere else.

✞ Making Straight Lines out of Crooked People ✞

Abraham was too old
Isaac was a daydreamer
Jacob was a liar
Leah was ugly
Joseph was abused
Moses had a s-s-s-stuttering problem
Gideon was afraid
Sampson had long hair and was a womanizer
Rahab was a prostitute
Jeremiah and Timothy were too young
David had an affair and was a murderer
Elijah was suicidal
Isaiah preached naked
Jonah ran from God
Naomi was a widow
Job went bankrupt
John the Baptist ate bugs
Peter denied Christ
The disciples fell asleep while praying
Martha was a worrywart
The Samaritan woman was divorced—more than once
Zaccheus was too small
Paul was too religious
Timothy had an ulcer
Lazarus was dead

✝ One Flaw in Women ✝

By the time the Lord made woman, He was into his sixth day of working overtime. An angel appeared and asked, "Why are You spending so much time on this one?"

The Lord answered, "Have you seen my spec sheet on her?"

"Spec sheet?" replied the perplexed angel.

The Lord elatedly ticked off woman's specifications:

> "Be completely washable, but not plastic,
>
> Consist of more than two hundred movable parts, all replaceable,
>
> Able to run on diet soft drinks and leftovers,
>
> Have a lap that can hold four children at one time,
>
> Possess a kiss that can cure anything from a scraped knee to a broken heart,
>
> Do everything with only two hands."

The angel was astounded at the requirements. "Only two hands? No way."

"And that's just on the standard model!" boasted the Lord.

"Lord, that's too much work for one day. Finish tomorrow," The angel advised.

"I cannot delay," the Lord protested. "I am so close to finishing this creation that is so close to My heart. She already heals herself when she is sick and can work eighteen-hour days."

The angel moved closer and touched the woman. "But You have made her so soft, Lord."

"She is soft," the Lord agreed, "but I have also made her tough. You have no idea what she can endure or accomplish."

"Will she be able to think?" questioned the angel.

The Lord replied, "Not only will she be able to think, she can reason and negotiate, too."

The angel noticed something, reached out, and touched the woman's cheek. "Oops, looks like You have a leak in this model. I knew You were trying to put too much into this one."

"That's not a leak," the Lord corrected, "That's a tear."

"What's the tear for?" the angel inquired.

The Lord answered, "The tear is her way of expressing her joy, her sorrow, her pain, her disappointment, her love, her loneliness, her grief, and her pride."

"How touching and sensitive she is, Lord," the angel offered. "But what makes her so close to Your heart?"

Beaming, the Lord responded, "I am glad you asked. I have endowed woman with a power that makes her exclusive among My entire creation."

"What is that, Lord?" inquired the puzzled angel.

"The ability to create human life; an ability that makes her most like Me," proclaimed the Lord.

Impressed, the angel granted, "You are a genius, Lord. You thought of everything. Woman is truly amazing."

That she is:

Women have strengths that astound men.

Women bear hardships and carry burdens.

Women hold happiness, love, and joy.

Women smile when they want to scream.

Women sing when they want to cry.

Women cry when they are happy.

Women laugh when they are nervous.

Women fight for what they believe in.

Women stand up to injustice.

Women do not take no for an answer when they know there is a better solution.

Women go without so their family can have.

Women go to the doctor with a frightened friend.

Women love unconditionally.

Women cry when their children excel.

Women cheer when their friends get awards.

Women are happy when they hear about a birth or a wedding.

Women have hearts that break when a friend dies.

Women grieve at the loss of a family member.

Women are strong when you think there is no strength left.

Women know that a hug and a kiss can heal a broken heart.

Women come in all shapes, sizes, and colors.

Women will drive, fly, walk, run, or e-mail you to show how much they care about you.

Women bring joy, hope, and love.

Women have compassion and ideals.

Women give moral support to their family and friends.

Women have vital things to say and everything to give.

Women have hearts that keep the world turning.

However, if there is one flaw in women, it is that they forget their worth.

✝ Guidance ✝

When I meditated on the word guidance, I noticed the ending, "dance." I remember reading that doing God's will is a lot like dancing. When two people try to lead, nothing feels right. The movement does not flow with the music and everything is uncomfortable and erratic.

When one discerns that and allows the other to lead, both bodies flow smoothly. One gives gentle cues, perhaps a nudge to the back or pressing lightly in one direction or another. It is as if two become one, moving in rhythm.

Dance takes surrender and attentiveness from one person and gentle guidance and skill from the other. My eyes returned to the word guidance. When I saw "G," I thought of God, followed by "U" and "I." God you and I dance.

As I lowered my head in prayer, I became willing to trust God to lead and guide me through each season of my life.

Spiritual Humor e-Soup *A Compilation of Amusing Messages from the Internet*

Trading Places

A man was sick and tired of going to work every day while his wife luxuriated at home. Wanting her to experience what he went through, he prayed, "Dear Lord, switch our bodies for a day." God, in his infinite wisdom, granted the wish.

The next morning, he awoke as a woman and cooked breakfast for his spouse, awakened the kids, prepared their clothes, fed them, packed their lunches, drove them to school, dropped off dirty clothes and picked up dry cleaning, stopped at the bank to make a deposit, shopped for groceries, drove home, put away groceries, paid bills, and balanced the checkbook.

He cleaned the cat's litter box and bathed the dog and since it was already 1:00 P.M., he hurried to make beds, do the laundry, dust and mop the kitchen floor, and vacuum the carpet so he could pick up the kids from school and had an argument with them on the way home.

He served snacks, organized homework, and watched TV while ironing. At 4:30, he peeled potatoes, washed vegetables for salad, breaded pork chops, and snapped fresh beans for supper.

After supper, he cleaned the kitchen, ran the dishwasher, folded laundry, bathed the kids, and put them to bed. At 9 P.M., though his daily chores were not finished, he went to bed exhausted, where he was expected to make love, which he managed without complaint.

Early the next day, he woke up and quickly knelt in prayer, "Lord, I don't know what I was thinking. I was so wrong to envy my wife for staying home all day. Please, oh please, trade us back to normal."

The Lord, in his infinite wisdom, replied, "My son, I believe you have learned your lesson and I will be happy to return you to a normal life.

"You'll have to wait nine months since your wife got you pregnant last night."

♱ Carrot, Egg, and Coffee ♱

A young woman moaned to her mother about her difficult life. She did not know how she was going to make it and wanted to give up. She was tired of struggling. It seemed as one problem was solved, a new one arose.

Her mother led her to the kitchen, filled three pots with water, and placed each on a high fire. They came to a boil rapidly. In the first, she placed carrots; the second, eggs; and the last, coffee. Without a word, she let them sit and boil.

After twenty minutes, she turned off the burners. She fished out the carrots and placed them in a bowl; removed the eggs and placed them in a bowl; and ladled out the coffee and poured it in a bowl. She asked her daughter, "Tell me what you see?"

"Carrots, eggs, and coffee," the daughter replied.

Her mother asked her to feel the carrots. She did and noted they were soft. She asked her to crack an egg. After peeling the shell, she observed the hard-boiled content. She asked her to sip the coffee and the daughter smiled as she tasted its richness.

The daughter queried, "What does it mean, Mother?"

Her mother explained, "Each object faced the same adversity, boiling water; but each reacted differently. The carrot went in strong, hard, and unrelenting; but after being subjected to boiling water, it softened and weakened. The egg had been fragile; its thin outer shell protected its liquid interior. But after sitting in boiling water, its yolk became hardened. The ground coffee beans were unique, however. After boiling in water, they changed the water.

"Which are you?" she challenged her daughter. "When adversity knocks on your door, how do you respond?

"Are you the carrot that seems strong, but with pain and heartache do you wilt and become soft and lose strength?

"Are you the egg that starts with a malleable heart, but changes with the heat? Do you have a fluid spirit, but after difficulty, have you become hard-boiled? Does your shell look the same, but on the inside are you bitter and tough with a stiff spirit and hardened heart?

"Are you like the coffee bean which actually changes hot water, the very circumstance that brings the pain? When the water gets hot, it releases its fragrance and flavor. If you are like the bean, when life is at its worst, you get better and change the environment around you.

"Are you a carrot, an egg, or a coffee bean?"

✝ Edith Easter ✝

Edith Burns, a faithful Christian, was a patient of Dr. Wil Phillips, a gentle doctor who saw patients as people. Edith was his favorite.

One morning, he went to his office with a heavy heart because of Edith. When he entered his waiting room, there she sat with her Bible in her lap, earnestly talking to a young mother.

Edith made a habit of introducing herself this way: "Hello, my name is Edith Burns. Do you believe in Easter?" She followed with an explanation of Easter. At times, people would be saved.

Dr. Phillips saw his head nurse, Beverly. When Beverly first met Edith to take her blood pressure, Edith began by saying, "My name is Edith Burns. Do you believe in Easter?"

Beverly said, "Why, yes, I do."

Edith said, "Wonderful, what do you believe about Easter?"

Beverly answered, "It's about egg hunts and dressing up to go to church." Edith pressed her about the true meaning of Easter and led her to a saving knowledge of Jesus Christ.

On this morning Dr. Phillips warned his nurse, "Beverly, don't call Edith yet. I believe there's another delivery taking place in the waiting room."

After being escorted to the doctor's office, Edith queried, "Dr. Wil, why are you so sad? Are you reading your Bible? Are you praying?"

He said gently, "Edith, I'm the doctor and you're the patient." With a heavy heart, he continued, "Your lab report shows you have cancer. Edith, you don't have very long to live."

Edith chided, "Shame on you, Wil Phillips. Why are you so sad? Do you think God makes mistakes? You've told me I'm going to see my precious Lord Jesus and my husband. You've told me I'm going to celebrate Easter forever and you're having difficulty giving me my ticket."

Dr. Phillips thought, Edith Burns, you're a singular woman.

Edith continued seeing Dr. Phillips. For CHRISTmas, the office was closed till January 3. That day, Edith called to say, "I'm going to be taking my story to the hospital, Wil. Since I'm nearing home, can you make sure they room ladies by me who need to know about Easter?"

The hospital honored her request and many women were saved. Everybody on the floor was so enthralled that they nicknamed her Edith Easter. Well, everyone except Phyllis Cross, the head nurse.

Phyllis wanted nothing to do with Edith "because she's a religious nut." Formerly a nurse in an army hospital, she had seen and heard it all. She was the original G.I. Jane: married three times, hard, cold, and everything by the book.

One shift, the nurse assigned to Edith was sick. Edith had the flu and Phyllis had to give her a shot. When she walked in, Edith had a big smile on her face and greeted, "Phyllis, God loves you, I love you and have been praying for you."

Phyllis retorted, "You can quit praying for me, it won't work. I'm not interested."

Edith said, "I'll keep praying and ask God not to take me home till you join the family."

Nurse Cross snapped, "You'll never die because it'll never happen," and curtly left the room.

Every day, Phyllis would enter and Edith would say, "Phyllis, God loves you, I love you and have been praying for you."

One day, Phyllis was drawn to Edith's room like a magnet attracts iron. She sat on the bed and Edith told her, "I'm so glad you've come, because God told me today is your special day."

Phyllis said, "Edith, you've asked everybody if they believe in Easter; but you never asked me."

Edith replied, "I wanted to but God told me to wait until you asked." Edith used her Bible to share the story of the death, burial, and resurrection of Jesus Christ. "Phyllis, do you believe in Easter? Do you believe that Jesus Christ is alive and that He wants to live in your heart?"

Phyllis prayed, "Oh, I believe it with all my heart and I want Jesus in my life." For the first time she did not walk out of a hospital room, she was carried out on the wings of angels.

Two days later, Phyllis came and Edith said, "Do you know what day it is?"

Phyllis answered joyfully, "Edith, it's Good Friday."

Edith stated, "Oh, no, for you every day is Easter. Happy Easter, Phyllis."

On Sunday, Phyllis bought a dozen lilies she wanted to give Edith to wish her a Happy Easter. When she entered the room, Edith was in bed with a sweet smile on her face, her Bible on her lap, and her hands in the Bible.

at moved nearer and realized she was dead. Her left hand was inserted at John 14:2: "In my Father's house are many mansions. I go to prepare a place for you; I will come again and receive you to Myself, that where I am, there you may be also."

Her right hand indexed to Revelation 21:4: "And God will wipe away every tear from their eyes, there shall be no more death nor sorrow, nor crying; and there shall be no more pain, for the former things have passed away."

Phyllis lifted her face toward heaven and, with tears streaming down her cheeks, cried, "Happy Easter, Edith, Happy Easter."

She walked out of the room directly to a table where two student nurses sat. She greeted, "My name is Phyllis Cross. Do you believe in Easter?"

✠ Sand and Stone ✠

Two friends were walking through the desert. At one point, they had an argument and one slapped the other in the face. The one who got slapped was hurt but, without a word, he wrote in the sand: "Today my best friend slapped me in the face."

They continued their journey until they found an oasis where they bathed. The one who had been slapped got stuck in the mire and was drowning but the friend saved him. After recovering, he inscribed on a stone: Today my best friend saved my life.

The one who had slapped and saved his friend asked, "After I hurt you, you wrote in the sand but, now, you inscribe on a stone, why?"

The other replied, "When someone hurts us we should write it in sand where winds of forgiveness can erase it. But, when someone does a good deed for us, we must engrave it in stone where no wind can erase it."

Learn to write your hurts in the sand and carve your blessings in stone.

✠ At Age . . . I Learned . . . ✠

. . . 4 . . . I like my teacher because she cries when we sing "Silent Night."

. . . 5 . . . our dog does not want to eat my broccoli either.

. . . 7 . . . when I wave to people in the country, they stop what they are doing and wave back.

. . . 9 . . . when I get my room exactly the way I like it, Mom makes me clean it up again.

. . . 12 . . . if you want to cheer yourself up, you should try cheering someone else up.

. . . 14 . . . although it is hard to admit, I am secretly glad my parents are strict with me.

. . . 15 . . . silent company is often more healing than words of advice.

. . . 24 . . . brushing my child's hair is one of life's great pleasures.

. . . 26 . . . wherever I go, the world's worst drivers have followed me there.

. . . 29 . . . if someone says something unkind about me, I must live so that no one will believe it.

. . . 30 . . . there are people who love you dearly but do not know how to show it.

. . . 42 . . . you can make someone's day by simply sending them a little note.

. . . 44 . . . the greater a person's sense of guilt, the greater their need to cast blame on others.

. . . 46 . . . children and grandparents are natural allies.

. . . 47 . . . no matter what happens or how bad it seems today, it will be better tomorrow.

. . . 48 . . . singing "Amazing Grace" can lift my spirits for hours.

. . . 49 . . . motel mattresses are better on the side away from the phone.

. . . 50 . . . you can tell a lot about a man by the way he handles three things: a rainy day, lost luggage, and tangled CHRISTmas tree lights.

. . . 51 . . . keeping a vegetable garden is worth a medicine cabinet full of pills.

. . . 52 . . . regardless of your relationship with your parents, you miss them after they die.

. . . 53 . . . making a living is not the same thing as making a life.

. . . 58 . . . if you want to do something beneficial for your children, improve your marriage.

. . . 61 . . . life sometimes gives you a second chance.

. . . 62 . . . you should not go through life with a catcher's mitt on both hands. You need to be able to throw something back.

. . . 64 . . . if you pursue happiness, it will elude you. But if you focus on family, the needs of others, and doing the best you can, happiness will find you.

. . . 65 . . . whenever I decide something with kindness, I usually make the right decision.

. . . 66 . . . everyone can use a prayer.

. . . 72 . . . even when I have pains, I do not have to be one.

. . . 82 . . . people love human touch: holding hands, a warm hug, or a friendly pat on the back. Reach out and touch someone.

. . . 90 . . . I still have a lot to learn.

✟ Are You an Angel? ✟

On the way home, my car sputtered and died. I barely managed to coast into a gas station, glad not to be blocking traffic and to have a warm spot to await the tow truck. Before I made the call, I observed a woman walk out of the quick mart, slip, and fall into a gas pump. I jogged out to see if she were okay.

When I arrived, it appeared she had been overcome more by sobs than the fall. With dark circles under her eyes, she was haggard for a young woman. She dropped a coin as I helped her. I picked it up and returned it to her. It was a nickel.

In that instant, the situation came into focus: the crying woman, the ancient car crammed with three kids, one in a car seat, and the gas pump reading $4.95.

I asked her if she were okay and if she needed help. She answered, "I don't want my kids to see me crying." So we stood on the side of the pump away from her car. She said she was driving cross country and that times were very hard for her.

I asked, "You were praying?" She backed away but I assured her I was not a fanatic. "He heard you and sent me." I swiped my card through the reader on the pump so she could fill up her car. I ran to the food mart and bought two bags of groceries, gift certificates, and a coffee.

She served food to the kids, who attacked it like wolves. She and I stood by the pump and talked. She said her boyfriend left two months ago and she had not been able to make ends meet.

In desperation, she phoned her parents with whom she had not spoken in years. They said she could live with them. She told the kids they were going to the grandparents for CHRISTmas, but not that they were going to live there.

I gave her my gloves, a hug, and prayed with her for safety on the road. As I headed to my car, she inquired, "Are you an angel?"

Her question brought tears to my eyes. "Sweetie, angels are busy this time of year, so God uses regular people."

It was unbelievable to be part of someone's miracle. Of course, when I got in my car, it started right away and carried me home uneventfully. I will put it in the shop but suspect the mechanic will find nothing wrong.

Sometimes angels fly close enough that you can hear the flutter of their wings.

✝ Bury Me with a Fork in My Hand ✝

A young woman diagnosed with a terminal illness was given three months to live. Putting her affairs in order, she discussed with her pastor which hymns she wanted sung at the service, scriptures read, and outfit to be buried in. The pastor was preparing to leave when the young woman suddenly remembered. "There's one more important thing," she said excitedly.

"What's that?" the pastor replied.

"I want to be buried with a fork in my hand." The pastor stared at the young woman, not knowing what to say.

"That surprises you, doesn't it?" the young woman asked.

"Well, honestly, I'm puzzled by the request," replied the pastor, candidly.

She explained. "My grandmother told me a story and I have tried to pass along its message to those I love and those in need of encouragement:

"'In all my years attending church socials and potluck dinners, I remember when the dishes of the main course were being cleared, someone would inevitably say, "Keep your fork." It was my favorite part because I knew that something wonderful was coming like velvety chocolate cake or deep-dish apple pie.'"

She continued, "So, I want people to see me in that casket with a fork in my hand and I want them to wonder, *What's with the fork?* During the service, I'd like you to encourage them, 'Keep your fork, the best is yet to come.'"

The pastor's eyes welled up with tears of joy as he hugged the young woman good-bye. He knew this would be the last time he would see her before her death. He also realized that she had a better grasp of heaven than he did.

At the funeral, people paying their respects saw the pretty dress she was wearing and the fork in her hand. Over and over, the pastor heard, "What's with the fork?" Over and over he smiled.

During his sermon, the pastor repeated the conversation he had with the young woman before she died. The pastor related how he could not stop thinking about the fork and those who witnessed it probably would not be able to stop thinking about it either.

The next time you reach for your fork, let it remind you, "The best is yet to come."

✟ By the Grace of God ✟

A man dies and arrives at the pearly gates. St. Peter greets him, "Here's how it works. You need one hundred points to get into heaven. Tell me the good deeds you've done, and I award you points for each depending on how good it was. When you reach one hundred, you get in."

"Okay," the man agrees, "I was married to the same woman for fifty years and never cheated on her, even in my heart."

"That's wonderful," says St. Peter, "that's worth three points."

"Only three?" the man exclaims. "Well, I attended church my entire life and supported its ministry with my time, talent, and tithe."

"Terrific," offers St. Peter. "That's certainly worth a point."

"One point?" the man squeals. "I started a soup kitchen in my city and worked in a shelter for homeless veterans."

"Fantastic, that's good for two more points," Peter reports.

"Two points." Exasperated, the man cries, "At this rate, the only way I'll get into heaven is by the grace of God."

"Bingo, one hundred points. Come on in."

✝ Oh God, Forgive Me When I Whine ✝

Today, on a bus, I saw a beautiful woman
And wished I were as beautiful.
When suddenly she rose to leave,
I saw her hobble down the aisle.
She had one leg and carried a crutch.
But as she passed, she paused to smile.
Oh God, forgive me when I whine.
I have two legs. The world is mine.

I stopped to buy some candy.
The lad who sold it had such charm.
I talked with him, he seemed so glad.
If I were late, it'd do no harm.
And as I left, he said to me, "I thank you, you've been so kind.
It's nice to talk with folks like you. You see," he said, "I'm blind."
Oh God, forgive me when I whine.
I have two eyes. The world is mine.

Later, while walking down the street, I saw a child I knew.
He stood and watched the others play, but did not know what to do.
I stopped a moment and said, "Why don't you join them, dear?"
He looked ahead without a word. I forgot, he couldn't hear.
Oh God, forgive me when I whine.
I have two ears. The world is mine.

With feet to take me where I'd go.
With eyes to see the sunset's glow.
With ears to hear what I'd know.
Oh God, forgive me when I whine.
I've been blessed indeed. The world is mine.

Spiritual Humor e-Soup — A Compilation of Amusing Messages from the Internet

Heavenly Spelling Bee

Husband John and wife Carla are in a car accident. John dies immediately, goes to heaven, and meets Peter at the gate of Heaven. Peter greets him by name and asks him to spell "dog." He spells dog correctly and Peter opens the door.

As he enters, Peter says, "John, I have to visit the restroom. Can you stand guard while I'm gone?"

John replies, "Yes, of course." Peter leaves.

Thirty seconds later, John's wife arrives. She is surprised to see her husband at the gate.

Husband: "Carla honey, what happened?"

Wife: "Because of your lousy driving, I died in the ambulance on the way to the hospital." She inquires, "What are you doing at the gate, John?"

Husband; "Peter left me in charge."

Wife: "Well, can I enter?"

Husband: "Sure, but you have to spell a word first."

Wife: "A spelling bee? What word?"

Husband: "Supercalifragilisticexpialidocious."

✠ The Cross ✠

A young man was at the end of his rope, seeing no way out; he dropped to his knees. "Lord, I can't go on," he said. "I have too heavy a cross to bear."

The Lord replied, "My son, if you can't bear its weight, place your cross inside this room. Then, open the other door and select any cross you wish."

Filled with relief, the man said, "Thank you, Lord," and did as he was directed. Entering the other room, he saw many crosses; some so large the tops were not visible. He spotted a tiny cross leaning against a far wall.

Pointing, he whispered, "I'd like that one, Lord."

The Lord replied, "My son, that is the cross you brought in."

Whatever your cross, whatever your pain,
There will always be sunshine after the rain.
Perhaps you may stumble, perhaps even fall.
But God's always there to help you through it all.

✟ If Only There Were More Like Him ✟

Your alarm goes off; you hit "snooze" and take an extra ten minutes.
He stays up for days on end.

You take a warm shower to help you wake up.
He goes days or weeks without running water.

You complain of a headache and call in sick.
He gets shot at, as others are hit, and keeps moving forward.

You put on your "anti-war/don't support the troops" shirt and meet up with your friends.
He still fights for your right to wear that shirt.

You make sure your cell phone is in your pocket.
He clutches the cross hanging on his chain next to his dog tags.

You talk trash on your buddies that are not with you.
He knows he may not see some of his buddies again.

You walk down the beach, staring at all the pretty girls.
He walks the streets, searching for insurgents and terrorists.

You complain about how hot it is.
He wears heavy gear, not daring to remove his helmet to wipe his brow.

You complain because the restaurant got your order wrong.
He does not get to eat today.

Your maid makes your bed and washes your clothes.
He wears the same garb for months, but makes sure his weapons are clean.

You go to the mall and get your hair done.
He does not have time to brush his teeth today.

You are angry because your class ran five minutes over.
He is told he will be held over an extra two months.

You call your girlfriend and set a date for that night.
He waits for the mail to see if there is a letter from home.

You hug and kiss your girlfriend every day.
He holds his letter close and smells his love's perfume.

You roll your eyes as a baby cries.
He gets a letter with pictures of his new child and wonders if they will ever meet.

You criticize your government and say that war never solves anything.
He sees the innocent tortured and killed by their government and remembers why he is fighting.

You tell jokes about the war and make fun of men like him.
He hears gunfire and bombs.

You see only what the media wants you to see.
He sees the bodies lying around him.

You are asked to go to the store by your parents. You refuse.
He does what he is told without question or delay.

You watch TV or listen to music on your iPod in your home.
He takes whatever time is allotted to call or write home, sleep, or eat.

You crawl into bed with down pillows and nestle in comfort.
He crawls under a tank for shade and a five-minute nap only to be awakened by gunfire.

You judge him by claiming the world is worse off because of men like him.
If only there were more like him.

♱ Your Red Rose ♱

Each year he sent her roses and the note would always say,
"I love you even more this year than last year on this day.
My love for you will always grow with every passing year."

She knew this was the last time that the roses would appear.
She thought he ordered roses in advance before this day.
Her loving husband did not know that he would pass away.

He always liked to do things early, way before the time.
Then, if he got too busy, everything would work out fine.
She trimmed the stems and placed them in a very special vase,
Then set the vase beside the portrait of his smiling face.

She would sit for hours in her husband's favorite chair,
While staring at his picture and the roses sitting there.
A year went by and it was to live without her mate
With loneliness and solitude that had become her fate.

Then, the very hour, the doorbell rang,
And there were roses sitting by her door.
She brought the roses in and looked at them in shock.
Then went to get the telephone to call the florist shop.

The owner answered and she asked, "Would you please explain,
Why would someone do this, causing me such pain?"
"I know your husband passed away more than a year ago, so
I knew you'd call and you would want to know.

"The flowers you received today were paid for in advance.
Your husband always planned ahead, he left nothing to chance.
There is a standing order that I have on file down here,
And he has paid, well in advance; you'll get them every year.

"There also is another thing, that I think you should know
He wrote a special little card, he did this years ago.
Then, should ever I find out that he's no longer here,
That's the card that should be sent to you the following year."

She thanked him and hung up the phone, her tears flowing hard,
Her fingers shaking as she slowly reached to get the card.
Inside the card, she saw that he had written her a note.
Then, as she stared in total silence, she read what he wrote . . .

"Hello, my love, I know it's been a year since I've been gone.
I hope it hasn't been too hard for you to overcome.
I know it must be lonely and the pain is very real.
'Cause if it was the other way, I know just how I would feel.

"The love we shared made everything so beautiful in life.
I loved you more than words can say, you were the perfect wife.
You were my friend and lover, you fulfilled my every need.
I know it's only been a year but please try not to grieve.

"I want you to be happy, even when you shed your tears.
That is why the roses will be sent to you for years.
When you get these roses, think of all the happiness
That we had together and how both of us were blessed.

"I have always loved you and I know I always will.
But, my love, you must go on, you have some living still.
Please try to find happiness while living out your days.
I know it is not easy but I hope you find some ways.

"The roses will come every year and they will only stop
If your door's not answered when the florist stops to knock.
He will come five times that day, in case you have gone out.
But after his last visit, he will know without a doubt
To take the roses to the place where I've instructed him,
And place the roses where we are, together once again."

✢ Truths to Ponder ✢

1 Faith is the ability to not panic.

2. If you worry, you didn't pray. If you pray, don't worry.

3. For a child of God, prayer is kind of like calling home every day.

4. Blessed are the flexible, for they shall not be bent out of shape.

5. When we get tangled up in our problems, we must be still so God can untangle the knot.

6. Do the math. Count your blessings.

7. God wants spiritual fruit, not religious nuts.

8. Dear God: I have a problem. It's me.

9. Silence is often misinterpreted, but never misquoted.

10. Laugh every day; it's like inner jogging.

11. The most important things in your home are the people.

12. Growing old is inevitable, growing up is optional.
13. There is no key to happiness. The door is always open.
14. A grudge is a heavy burden to carry.
15. He who dies with the most toys is still dead.
16. We do not remember days, but moments. Life moves fast, so enjoy your precious moments.
17. Nothing is real to you until you experience it, otherwise it's hearsay.
18. It's all right to sit on your pity pot every now and again. Be sure to flush when you are done.
19. Surviving and living your life successfully requires courage. The goals and dreams you are seeking require courage and risk-taking. Learn from the turtle: It only makes progress when it sticks out its neck.
20. Be more concerned with your character than your reputation, because your character is what you really are, while your reputation is merely what others think you are.
21. Feed your faith and your doubts will starve to death.

✟ He Sits as a Refiner and Purifier of Silver ✟

—Malachi 3:3

This verse puzzled a women's Bible study group. They wondered what the statement meant about the character and nature of God. One woman offered to research the process of refining silver and report at the next session.

She made an appointment with a silversmith to watch him work, but did not mention the reason for her interest beyond a curiosity about refining silver.

As she observed, the silversmith explained, "To refine silver, you hold it in the middle of the fire where the flames are hottest to burn away all the impurities."

The woman thought about God holding us in such a hot spot and pondered the verse, *He sits as a refiner and purifier of silver.*

She inquired, "Is it true that you have to sit in front of the fire the whole time the silver is being refined?"

He said, "Yes, not only do I sit here holding the silver, I have to keep my eyes on it the entire time it's in the fire. If silver is left in the flames an instant too long, it is destroyed."

A moment later, she asked, "How do you know when the silver is fully refined?"

He grinned and replied, "That's easy. When I see my image in it."

If you are feeling the heat of the fire, remember that God has His eye on you and will keep watching you until He sees His image.

✟ What's in a Deck of Cards? ✟

It was a quiet day. The guns, mortars, and bombs, for some reason, had been silent. The young soldier knew it was Sunday, the holiest day of the week. Sitting alone, he pulled out an old deck of cards and spread them across his bunk. A sergeant came in and asked, "Why aren't you with the rest of the platoon?"

The soldier replied, "I thought I'd stay behind and spend some time with the Lord."

The sergeant said, "Looks to me like you're playing cards."

The soldier responded, "No, sir. You see, since we're not allowed to have Bibles or other Christian material in this country, I talk to the Lord by studying this deck of cards."

The sergeant asked in disbelief, "How do you do that?"

The soldier replied reverently:

"The Ace reminds me that there is only one God.

"The Two represents the books of the Bible, Old and New Testaments.

"The Three denotes the Triune God: Father, Son, and Holy Spirit.

"The Four stands for the Gospels: Matthew, Mark, Luke, and John.

"The Five is for the virgins that were ten but only five were lauded.

"The Six is for the days it took God to create Heaven and Earth.

"The Seven is for the day God rested after making His Creation.

"The Eight is for the family of Noah, his wife, their three sons and wives; the people God spared from the flood that destroyed the earth.

"The Nine is for the lepers that Jesus cleansed. He healed ten but nine never thanked Him.

"The Ten represents the commandments that God handed down to Moses on tablets of stone.

"The Jack is a reminder of Satan, one of God's first angels, who got kicked out of heaven for his wicked ways and became the joker of eternal hell.

"The Queen stands for the Virgin Mary, Mother of Jesus.

"The King stands for Jesus, King of kings.

"When I count the dots on the cards, I come up with 365; one for every day of the year.

"There are a total of fifty-two cards in a deck: each a week, fifty-two in a year.

"The four suits represent the seasons: spring, summer, fall and winter.

"Each suit has thirteen cards: the thirteen weeks in a quarter.

"When I want to talk to God and thank Him, I pull out this old deck of cards that reminds me of what I have to be thankful for."

The sergeant, stunned, with tears in his eyes and pain in his heart, stammered, "Soldier, may I borrow your deck of cards?"

✠ Old Shoe Man ✠

I showered, shaved, and adjusted my tie.
I got there and sat in a pew just in time.
Bowing my head in prayer as I closed my eyes,
I saw the shoe of the man next to me touching my own. I sighed.

With plenty of room on either side, I thought, *Why must our soles touch?*
It bothered me, his shoe touching mine, but it didn't bother him much.
A prayer began: and I thought, *This man with the shoes has no pride.*
They're dusty, worn, and scratched. Even worse, there are holes on the side.

The prayer went on. The shoe man uttered a soft amen.
I tried to focus on the prayer but my thoughts were on his shoes again.
Aren't we supposed to look our best when walking through that door?
"Well, this certainly isn't it," I thought, glancing toward the floor.

Then the prayer was ended and the songs of praise began.
The shoe man was certainly loud, sounding proud as he sang.
His voice lifted the rafters, his hands were raised high.
The Lord could surely hear the shoe man's voice from the sky.

It was time for the offering and what I threw in was steep.
I watched as the shoe man reached into his pockets so deep.
I saw what was pulled out, what the shoe man put in.
Then I heard a soft "clink" as when silver hits tin.

The sermon really bored me to tears, and that's no lie.
It was the same for the shoe man, for tears fell from his eyes.
At the end of the service, as is the custom here,
We must greet new visitors and show them good cheer.

But I felt moved somehow and wanted to meet the shoe man.
So after the closing prayer, I reached over and shook his hand.
He was old and his skin was dark, and his hair was truly a mess,
But I thanked him for coming, for being our guest.

He said, "My name's Charlie. I'm glad to meet you, my friend."
There were tears in his eyes, but he had a large, wide grin.
"Let me explain," he said, wiping tears from his eyes.
"I've been coming here for months and you're the first to say 'Hi.'"

"I know that my appearance is not like all the rest,
But I really do try to always look my best.
I always clean and polish my shoes before my very long walk.
But by the time I get here, they're dirty and dusty, like chalk."

My heart filled with pain and I swallowed to hide my tears
As he continued to apologize for daring to sit so near.
He said, "When I get here, I know I must look a sight.
But I thought if I could touch you, then maybe our souls might unite."

I was silent for a moment knowing whatever was said
Would pale in comparison, so I spoke from my heart, not my head.
"Oh, you've touched me," I said, "and taught me, in part,
That the best of any man is what is found in his heart."

The rest, I thought, this shoe man will never know.
Like how thankful I really am that his dirty old shoe touched my soul.

✟ I Love You ✟

One morning you will never wake up. Do all your friends know you love them? I was thinking I could die at any time and wondered if I had any wounds needing to be healed, friendships needing to be rekindled, or three precious words needing to be said.

Let your family and friends know you love them, even if you think they do not love you. You would be amazed at what those three little words can accomplish.

In case God calls me home before I see you again, "I love you."

✟ They Won't Let Me In Either ✟

A dog followed his owner to school. His owner was a fourth grader at a public school. When the bell rang, the dog slipped inside the building. He made it to the child's classroom before a teacher noticed and shooed him outside, slamming the door behind him.

The dog sat down, whimpered, and stared at the closed doors. God appeared beside the dog, patted his head, and bemoaned, "Don't feel bad, fella', they won't let Me in either."

✝ Scriptural Rules from God ✝

1. *Wake up and decide to have a good day.*

"Today is the day the Lord hath made; let us rejoice and be glad in it." *Psalms 118:24*

2. *Dress up by putting on a smile. A smile is an inexpensive way to improve your looks.*

"The Lord does not look at the things man looks at. Man looks at outward appearance; but the Lord looks at the heart." *I Samuel 16:7*

3. *Shut up, say nice things, and learn to listen. God gave us two ears and one mouth; so, He meant for us to do twice as much listening as talking.*

"He who guards his lips guards his soul." *Proverbs 13:3*

4. *Stand up for what you believe in. Stand for something or you will fall for anything.*

"Let us not be weary in doing good; for at the proper time, we will reap a harvest if we do not give up. Therefore, as we have opportunity, let us do good." *Galatians 6:9-10*

5. *Look up to the Lord.*

"I can do everything through Christ who strengthens me." *Philippians 4:13*

6. *Reach up for something higher.*

"Trust in the Lord with all your heart, and lean not unto your own understanding. In all your ways, acknowledge Him, and He will direct your path." *Proverbs 3:5-6*

7. *Lift up your prayers.*

"Do not worry about anything; instead pray about everything." *Philippians 4:6*

☩ From Fasting to Feasting ☩

Fast from judging others; feast on seeing the best in people.

Fast from emphasis on differences; feast on the unity of life.

Fast from despair; feast on hope.

Fast from thoughts of illness; feast on the healing power of God.

Fast from words that destroy; feast on phrases that encourage.

Fast from discontent; feast on gratitude.

Fast from worry; feast on trust.

Fast from complaining; feast on appreciation.

Fast from anger; feast on patience.

Fast from being negative; feast on being positive.

Fast from hostility; feast on peacemaking.

Fast from bitterness; feast on forgiveness.

Fast from constant activity; feast on slowing down.

Fast from disrespect; feast on recognizing the sacred in all life.

Fast from self-concern; feast on compassion for others.

✟ The Lamb ✟

Mary had a little Lamb,
His fleece was white as snow.
And everywhere that Mary went,
The Lamb was sure to go.

He followed her to school each day,
'Twasn't even in the rule.
It made the children laugh and play,
To have a Lamb at school.

And then the rules all changed one day,
Illegal it became
To bring the Lamb of God to school,
Or even speak His Name.

Every day got worse and worse,
And days turned into years.
Instead of hearing children laugh,
We heard gunshots and tears.

What must we do to stop the crime
That's in our schools today?
Let's let the Lamb come back to school,
And teach our kids to pray.

✟ For Whom the Bell Tolls ✟

Up the road from my home is a field with two horses. From a distance, they look like any other horses. But if you go closer, you will notice something quite remarkable.

Peering into the eyes of the larger horse, you will discover that he is blind. The owner has chosen not to put him down but, instead, has made a good home for him. This alone is amazing.

While nearby, you will hear the sound of a bell and detect that it comes from the smaller horse. Attached to her halter is a bell that tells her blind friend where she is, so he can follow.

As you observe, you will notice her checking on him and him loyally listening for her bell. He saunters to where she is, trusting she will not lead him astray. When returning to the barn, she stops regularly to glance back and make sure her friend is not too far away to hear her bell.

Like the owner of these horses, God does not throw us away because we are imperfect or have problems. He watches over us and brings others into our lives to help us when we are in need.

Sometimes we are the blind horse being guided by the ringing bell. At other times, we are the guide horse helping others see.

Good friends are like this. You do not always see them, but you know they are there. Listen for my bell and I will listen for yours.

✟ A Little Greeting ✟

This little greeting I'm sending your way
Hoping that maybe I'll brighten your day.

With it comes happiness, love, and good cheer,
Wishing you laughter, throughout the whole year.

Not a tear in your eye, but a smile on your face,
One that's so bright it can light the darkest place.

Laughter ringing, so loud and so true
That no one around you could ever be blue.

Just remember these wishes I'm sending your way,
Just hoping that maybe you'll have a nice day.

♰ The Marine ♰

We all came together, both young and old,
To fight for our freedom, to stand and be bold.
In the midst of all evil, we stand our ground,
And we protect our country from all terror around.

Peace and not war is what some people say.
But I'll give my life so you can live the American way.
I give you the right to talk of your peace,
To stand in your groups and protest in our streets.

But still I fight on, I don't bitch, I don't whine.
I'm merely one of the people who is doing your time.
I'm harder than nails, stronger than any machine.
I'm the immortal soldier, I'm a U.S. Marine.

So stand in my shoes, and leave from your home.
Fight for people who hate you, with protests they've shown.
Fight for the stranger, fight for the young,
So they all may have the greatest freedom you've won.

Fight for the sick, fight for the poor,
Fight for the cripple who lives next door.
But when your time comes, do what I've done.
If you stand up for freedom, you'll stand when the fight's done.

Corporal Aaron M. Gilbert
U.S. Marine Corps
U.S.S. Saipan, Persian Gulf

March 23, 2003

Hey Dad,

Do me a favor and label this "The Marine" and forward it to your contact list. Leave this letter in it. I want this rolling across the U.S., every home reading it, every eye seeing it, and every heart to feel it. So can you, please, forward this for me? I would but my personal time isn't that long and I don't have much time anyway.

You know what, Dad? I wondered what it would be like to truly understand what J.F.K. said in his inaugural address at Yale Law School when he stated, "Only a few generations have been granted the role of defending freedom in its hour of maximum danger. I do not shrink from this responsibility. I welcome it."

Well, now I know. And I do. Dad, I welcome the opportunity to do what I do. Even though I have left behind a beautiful wife, and I will miss the birth of our firstborn child, I would do it seventy times over to fight for the place that God has made for my home.

I love and miss you all very much. I wish I could be there when Sandi has our baby, but tell her that I love her, and Lord willing, I will be coming home soon. Give Mom a great big hug from me and give one to yourself, too.

Aaron

Visit this website: www.letssaythanks.com

⸸ Best and Worst Traits ⸸

The most destructive habit: worry

The greatest joy: giving

The greatest loss: self-respect

The most satisfying work: helping others

The ugliest personality trait: selfishness

The most endangered species: dedicated leaders

Our greatest natural resource: our youth

The greatest motivation: encouragement

The greatest problem to overcome: fear

The most effective sleeping pill: peace of mind

The most crippling disease: excuses

The most powerful force in life: love

The most dangerous pariah: a gossiper

The world's most incredible computer: the brain

The worst thing to be without: hope

The deadliest weapon: the tongue

The two most power-filled words: I can

The greatest asset: faith

The most worthless emotion: self-pity

The most beautiful attire: smile

The most prized possession: integrity

The most powerful channel of communication: prayer

The most contagious spirit: enthusiasm

✟ I Still Know Who She Is ✟

On a busy morning around 8:30 A.M., a gentleman in his eighties arrived to have stitches removed from his thumb. He said he was in a hurry as he had another appointment at 9:00 A.M.

I checked his vital signs and led him to a seat, knowing it would be an hour before someone would attend to him. I noticed him checking his watch and decided I would evaluate his wound. On exam, it was well healed, so I informed a doctor and gathered the supplies to remove his sutures and redress his wound.

While caring for him, we conversed. I asked if he had another doctor's appointment since he was in a hurry. He said no; he needed to go to the nursing home to eat breakfast with his wife.

I inquired about her health. He informed me she had been there a while and was a victim of Alzheimer's. I asked if she would be upset if he were late. He replied that she no longer knew who he was; she had not recognized him for the past five years.

Amazed, I asked, "You still go every morning, even though she doesn't know who you are?"

He smiled as he patted my hand kindly and replied, "She doesn't know me, but I still know who she is."

Holding back tears and experiencing goose bumps on my arms, I thought, *That is the kind of love I want in my life.*

True love is neither physical, nor romantic,
but an acceptance of all that is, has been, will be, and will not be.

✟ Man in the Glass ✟

When you get what you want in your struggle for self
And the world makes you king for a day,
Go to the mirror and look at yourself
And see what that man has to say.

For it isn't your father or mother or wife
Whose judgment upon you must pass.
The fellow whose verdict counts most in life
Is the one staring back from the glass.

You may be like Jack Horner and chisel a plum
And think you're a wonderful guy,
But the man in the glass says you're only a bum
If you can't look him straight in the eye.

He's the fellow to please, never mind all the rest,
For he's with you clear to the end.
And you've passed your most difficult test
If the man in the glass is your friend.

You may fool all the world down the pathway of years
And get pats on the back as you pass,
But your final reward will be heartache and tears
If you've cheated the man in the glass.

✟ Things to Remember ✟

Your presence is a present to the world.
You're unique and one of a kind.
Your life can be what you want it to be.
Take the days just one at a time.

Count your blessings, not your troubles.
You'll make it through whatever comes along.
Within you are so many answers.
Understand, have courage, be strong.

Don't put limits on yourself.
So many dreams are waiting to be realized.
Decisions are too important to leave to chance.
Reach for your peak, your goal, and your prize.

Nothing wastes more energy than worrying.
The longer one carries a problem, the heavier it gets.

Don't take things too seriously.
Live a life of serenity, not a life of regrets.

Remember that a little love goes a long way.
Remember that a lot of love goes forever.
Remember that friendship is a wise investment.
Life's treasures are people together.

Realize it's never too late.
Take the time to wish upon a star.
And don't ever forget for even a day
How very special you truly are.

Lessons on Life

A father wanted his four sons to learn not to judge things too quickly. He sent them on a quest, in turn, to view a pear tree that was a great distance away.

The first son journeyed in winter, the second in spring, the third in summer, and the youngest in fall. After, he called them together to describe what they had seen.

The first son expressed, "The tree was ugly, bent, and twisted."

The second son, "No, it was covered with green buds and full of promise."

The third, "It was laden with blossoms that smelled so sweet and looked so beautiful. It was the most graceful sight I've ever seen."

The youngest, "It was ripe and drooping with fruit, full of life and fulfillment."

The man explained, "Each of you is correct, because you have seen but only one season in the life of the tree.

"You cannot judge a tree or a person by one season. The essence of who they are, the joy, pleasure, and love that life produces, can only be measured at the end, when the seasons are over.

"If you give up in winter, you will miss the promise of your spring, the beauty of your summer, the fulfillment of your fall. Do not permit the pain of one season to destroy the joy of the rest. Persevere through the thorny patches and better times are sure to come."

⸸ Are You an Old Barn? ⸸

A stranger came by to make an offer that set me to thinking. He wanted to buy the old barn that sits out by the highway. I told him he was crazy. He was a city type: You could tell by his clothes, car, hands, and accent.

He said he was passing by and noticed the beautiful barn sitting in the tall grass and wanted to know if it was for sale.

I told him he had a funny idea of beauty. It was a nice-looking structure in its day but it had seen many winters with snow, ice, and howling winds. The summer sun had beaten down till the paint was gone and the wood had turned silver-gray. The old, leaning shack appeared somewhat tired. Yet, that fellow called it beautiful.

And that set me to thinking. I walked to the field and gazed upon that aged barn. The stranger intended to use the lumber to line the walls of the den in his new country home. He said you could not buy paint that exquisite. Only years of bearing storms and scorching sun can produce wood that magnificent.

Then it hit me. We are like that barn wood, but it is on the inside that the beauty grows. We turn silver-gray too and lean more than when we were young and full of sap. But the Lord knows what He is doing. As the years pass, He is busy using the hard wealth of our lives, the dry spells and stormy seasons, to beautify our souls the way nothing else can.

Today, they took the old barn down and hauled it away to decorate a rich man's home. I reckon someday we will be hauled off to take on whatever chores the good Lord has planned for us in the Great Country Home in the sky.

I suspect we will be more striking for the seasons we have been through and maybe add a touch of beauty to our Father's eternal home.

⸸ You Say, God Says ⸸

You say: "It's impossible."
God says: "All things are possible." Luke 18:27

You say: "I'm too tired."
God says: "I will give you rest." Matthew 11:28-30

You say: "Nobody really loves me."
God says: "I love you." John 3:16

You say: "I can't go on."
God says: "My grace is sufficient." II Corinthians 12:9 and Psalm 91:15

You say: "I can't figure things out."
God says: "I will direct your steps." Proverbs 3:5-6

You say: "I can't do it."
God says: "You can do all things." Philippians 4:13

You say: "I'm not able."
God says: "I am able." II Corinthians 9:8

You say: "It's not worth it."
God says: "It will be worth it." Romans 8:28

You say: "I can't forgive myself."
God says: "I forgive you." Romans 8:1

You say: "I can't manage."
God says: "I will supply all your needs." Philippians 4:19

You say: "I'm afraid."
God says: "I have not given you a spirit of fear." II Timothy 1:7

You say: "I'm always worried and frustrated."
God says: "Cast all your cares on Me." I Peter 5:7

You say: "I'm not smart enough."
God says: "I give you wisdom." I Corinthians 1:30

You say: "I feel all alone."
God says: "I will never leave you or forsake you." Hebrews 13:5

✝ Find Thirty Books of the Bible ✝

There are thirty books of the Bible on this page. Can you find them? This is a most remarkable puzzle. It was found by a gentleman in an airplane seat pocket, on a flight from Los Angeles to Honolulu, keeping him occupied for hours.

He enjoyed it so much, he passed it on to some friends. One friend from Illinois worked on this while fishing from his john boat. Another friend studied it while playing his banjo. Elaine Taylor, a columnist friend, was so intrigued by it she mentioned it in her weekly newspaper column. Another friend judges the job of solving this puzzle so involving, she brews a cup of tea to help her nerves.

There will be some names that are really easy to spot. That's a fact. Some people, however, will soon find themselves in a jam; especially since the book names are not necessarily capitalized.

Truthfully, from answers we get, we are forced to admit it usually takes a minister or scholar to see some of them at the worst. Research has shown that something in our genes is responsible for the difficulty we have in seeing the books in this paragraph.

During a recent fundraising event that featured this puzzle, the Alpha Delta Phi lemonade booth set a new sales record. The local paper, *The Chronicle,* surveyed over two hundred patrons who reported that this puzzle was one of the most difficult they had ever seen.

As Daniel Humana humbly puts it, "The books are all right here in plain view hidden from sight." Those able to find all of them will hear great lamentations from those who have to be shown.

One revelation that may help is that books like Timothy and Samuel may occur without their numbers. Also, keep in mind that punctuation and spaces in the middle are normal. A chipper attitude will help you compete really well against those who claim to know the answers. Remember, there is no need for a mad exodus, there really are thirty books of the Bible lurking somewhere on this page waiting to be found.

For answer key, go to: www.e-soupministry.com or telephone: (847) 606-8854.

✝ When We Are Down, God Is Up to Something ✝

When we are tired and discouraged from fruitless effort,
God knows how hard we have tried.

When we have cried so long our heart is in anguish,
God has counted our tears.

When we feel that our life is on hold and time has passed us by,
God is waiting for us.

When nothing makes sense and we are confused or frustrated,
God has the answer.

If our outlook suddenly brightens and we find traces of hope,
God has whispered to us.

When things are going well and we have much to be thankful for,
God has blessed us.

When something joyful happens and fills us with awe,
God has smiled upon us.

Wherever you are or whatever you are feeling,
God knows.

✝ This Will Make You MADD ✝

I went to a party and remembered what you said.
You told me not to drink, Mom, so I sipped a cola instead.
I felt proud of myself, the way you said I would,
When I didn't drink and drive, though friends said I should.

I made a healthy choice, and your advice to me was right.
The party finally ended, and the kids drove out of sight.
I got into my car, sure to get home in one piece.
I never knew what was coming, Mom, something I expected least.

Now I'm lying on the pavement, and I hear the policeman say,
"The kid that caused this was drunk." His voice seems far away.
My own blood's all around me, as I try hard not to cry.
I can hear the paramedic say, "This girl is going to die."

I'm sure the guy had no idea, while he was flying high.
Because he chose to drink and drive, I would have to die.
Why do people do it, Mom, knowing that it ruins lives?
Now the pain is cutting me, like a hundred stabbing knives.

Tell Sister not to be afraid, Mom, tell Daddy to be brave.
When I go to heaven, put "Mommy's Girl" on my grave.
Someone should've taught him it's wrong to drink and drive.
Maybe if his parents had, I'd still be alive.

My breath is getting shorter, Mom, I'm really getting scared.
These are my final moments, and I'm so unprepared.
I wish that you could hold me, Mom, as I lie here and die.
I wish I could say, "I love you, Mom," and kiss you, "Bye-bye."

✦ Where Were You on 9/11? ✦

You say you will never forget where you were when you heard the news on September 11, 2001. Neither will I.

I was on the 110th floor in a smoke-filled room with a man who called his wife to say good-bye. I steadied his fingers as he dialed and granted him the peace to say, "Honey, I'm not going to make it, but it's okay, I'm ready to go."

I was with his wife as she fed the children breakfast. When he called, I held her up as she heard his words and realized he was not coming home that night.

I was in the twenty-third-floor stairwell when a woman cried out to Me for the very first time in her life. "I've been knocking on the door of your heart for fifty years," I said. "Of course, I'll show you the way home; you need only believe in Me."

I was at the base of the building with the priest ministering to the injured and devastated souls. I took him home to tend to his flock in Heaven. He heard my voice and answered.

I was on all four of the planes, in every seat, with every prayer. I was with the crew as they were overwhelmed. I was in the hearts of the believers, comforting and assuring them that their faith had saved them.

I was in Texas, Kansas, London, everywhere. I was standing next to you when you heard the terrible news. Did you sense Me?

I saw every face and knew every name though not all knew Me. Some met Me for the first time on the 86th floor. Some sought Me with their very last breath. Some could not hear Me calling to them through the smoke and flames, "Come to Me. This way. Take my hand." Some had never heard my voice before and a few chose, for the final time, to ignore Me.

But, I was there.

I did not place you in the Tower that day. You may not know why, but I do. However, if you were there in that explosive moment in time, would you have reached for Me?

September 11, 2001, was not the end of the journey for you. But someday your sojourn will end and I will be there for you as well. Seek Me while I may be found. Then, at any moment, you know you are "ready to go."

I will be in the stairwell of your final moments.

✝ Who Will Take the Son? ✝

A wealthy man and his son loved to collect rare art; they owned an assembly including everything from Picasso to Raphael. They would often sit together and admire the great works.

When the Vietnam conflict broke out, the son went to war. He was courageous and died in battle rescuing another soldier. The father grieved deeply for his only son.

Weeks later, right before CHRISTmas, there was a knock at the door. A young man stood in the doorway with a package in his hands. "Sir, you don't know me, but I'm the soldier your son gave his life for. He saved many lives that day, and he was carrying me to safety when a bullet struck him in the heart and he died instantly. He often talked about you and your love for art."

The young man proffered the package. "I know this isn't great; I'm not much of an artist. I think your son would have wanted you to have this."

The father opened the parcel to find his son's portrait, painted by the young man. He stared in awe at the way the artist had captured his son's personality. The father was so drawn to the eyes that his eyes filled with tears. He thanked the young man and offered to pay for the painting.

"Oh, no sir, I could never repay what your son did for me. It's a gift."

The father hung the portrait over his mantel. When visitors arrived, he presented the painting of his son before any of the great works he had collected.

When he died, there was to be a great auction of his art. Many influential people gathered, excited to view the famous works and have an opportunity to purchase one for their collection.

On the dais sat the painting of the son. The auctioneer pounded his gavel. "We will begin with this portrait of the son. Who will start the bidding?"

Silence ensued until a voice shouted, "We want to see the famous paintings. Skip this one."

The auctioneer continued. "Will somebody bid for this painting, please?"

Another voice, angrily, "We didn't come to see this one. We came to see the Van Goghs, the Rembrandts. Get on with the real bids."

The auctioneer persisted, "The son, the son. Who'll take the son?"

A voice hailed from the back of the room, the longtime gardener of the father. "I'll give $10 for the painting," a large amount for his financial status.

"We have $10. Who will bid $20?" the auctioneer encouraged.

"Give it to him for $10 and let's see the masters," shouted another.

"$10 is the bid. Won't someone bid $20?" the auctioneer pleaded.

The crowd was becoming impatient. They did not want the son. They wanted the more worthy art for their investment portfolios.

The auctioneer pounded the gavel. "Going once, twice, sold for $10."

A man in the second row bellowed, "Let's get on with the real art."

The auctioneer laid down his gavel. "The auction is over."

"What about the masterpieces?" gasped the audience.

"When called to conduct this auction, I was informed of a stipulation in the will that I was not allowed to reveal until this moment: Only the painting of the son would be auctioned. Whoever bought that portrait would inherit the entire estate, including the art.

"The man who takes the son gets everything."

✟ Do You Smell That? ✟

A cold March wind danced around in the dead of night as the doctor entered the small hospital room of Diana Blessing. She was still groggy from surgery. Her husband, David, held her hand as they braced for the latest news.

That afternoon, complications had forced Diana, only twenty-four weeks pregnant, to undergo an emergency Caesarean to deliver the couple's daughter, Dana Lu. At twelve inches long and weighing only one pound, nine ounces, they knew she was perilously premature. Still, the doctor's soft words dropped like bombs.

"I don't think she's going to make it," he said, as kindly as he could. "There's only a ten percent chance she will live through the night and, even then, if by some slim chance she does, her future could be a very cruel one."

Numb with disbelief, they listened as the doctor described the devastating problems Dana would likely face if she survived: never walk or talk, probably be blind, surely prone to other catastrophic conditions from cerebral palsy to complete mental retardation, and on and on.

"No, no," Diana uttered.

She and David had long dreamed of the day they would have a daughter along with their five-year-old son, Dustin, to become a family of four. Within a matter of hours, that dream was slipping away.

As those first days passed, a new agony set in. Because Dana's underdeveloped nervous system was essentially raw, the lightest kiss or caress only intensified her discomfort. They could not even cradle their tiny baby against their chests to offer the warmth and strength of their love. All they could do, as Dana struggled beneath the ultraviolet light in a tangle of tubes and wires, was to pray that Jesus would stay close to their precious little girl.

There was never a moment when Dana suddenly grew stronger. As weeks passed, she gained an ounce of weight here and an ounce of strength there. At last, when she turned two months old, her parents were able to hold her for the first time. Two months later, though doctors continued to gently but grimly warn that her chances of surviving, much less living any kind of normal life, were next to zero, Dana went home from the hospital, as her mother had predicted.

Five years later, Dana was a petite but feisty young girl with glittering gray eyes and an unquenchable zest for life. She showed no signs whatsoever of any mental or physical impairment. Clearly, she was everything a little girl can be and more.

But that happy ending is far from the end of her story.

One blistering summer afternoon, Dana was sitting in her mother's lap in the bleachers of a local ballpark where her brother Dustin's baseball team was practicing. As always, Dana was chattering nonstop with her mother and other adults nearby when she abruptly fell silent. Hugging her arms across her chest, little Dana asked, "Do you smell that?"

Smelling the air and detecting the approach of a storm, Diana said, "Yes, it smells like rain."

Dana closed her eyes and again asked, "Do you smell that?"

Her mother repeated, "Yes, I think we're about to get wet. It smells like rain."

Wrapped in the moment, Dana shook her head, patted her thin shoulders with her small hands, and stated, "No, it smells like Him. It smells like Jesus when you lay your head on His chest."

Tears blurred Diana's eyes as Dana happily hopped down to play with the other children. Her daughter's words confirmed what Diana and members of the extended Blessing family had known, at least in their hearts, all along.

During those long days and nights of her first two months of life, when her nerves were too sensitive for them to touch her, Jesus was holding Dana on His chest and it is His loving scent that she recalls so well.

Life is not measured by the breaths we take,
but by the moments that take our breath away.

✟ My Attorney ✟

After living a decent life, my time on earth came to a close. The next thing I recall is sitting on a bench in the waiting room of what appeared to be a courthouse. The doors opened and I was instructed to enter and take a seat at the defense table.

Peering around, I saw the prosecutor, a villainous-looking being, who snarled as he stared at me; definitely the most evil person I had ever seen. I peeked to my left and saw My Attorney, a kind, gentle-looking man whose appearance seemed familiar to me.

A door flew open and the Judge in flowing robes, an awesome presence, moved to the bench. I could not pry my eyes from Him. Taking His seat, He directed, "Let us begin."

The prosecutor arose, "My name is Satan and I'm here to prove this sinner belongs in hell." He proceeded to reveal the lies I told, things I stole, when I cheated, and perversions in my life. He unveiled sins I had conveniently forgotten. The more he spoke, the deeper I sank in my seat.

I was humiliated. But as upset as I was at Satan, I was more disturbed with My Attorney, who failed to offer any defense. I had been guilty of those sins, but I had done some good in my life. Did that not make up for part of the harm I had done?

Satan finished in a flurry, "This sinner belongs to me. He's guilty of the charges and there is no one who can refute me."

My Attorney asked to approach the bench. The Judge allowed this over a strong objection by Satan. As He walked to the bench, I saw His splendor and majesty. I realized Jesus, my Lord and Savior, was representing me.

At the bench, He said, "Hi, Dad," and turned to address the court. "Satan is correct; this man sinned. I won't deny the allegations. The wage of sin is death and this sinner deserves to be punished."

Jesus inhaled deeply and pivoted to His Father with outstretched arms and proclaimed, "However, I died on the cross so that he might have eternal life. He has repented and accepted Me as his Savior, so he is Mine."

My Lord continued, "His name is written in the Book of Life and no one can take him from Me. Satan still does not comprehend but this man is not to be given justice but, rather, mercy."

As Jesus sat, He paused, looked to His Father, and concluded, "There is nothing else that needs to be done. I've done it all."

The Judge lifted His mighty hand and slammed the gavel. These words resounded from His lips, "This man is free. The penalty for him has been paid in full. Case dismissed."

As my Lord embraced me and led me away, I could hear Satan ranting and raving, "I won't give up. I will win the next one."

I asked Jesus, "Have you ever lost a case?"

Christ smiled lovingly and replied, "Everyone who has come to Me has received the same verdict as you: 'Paid in Full.'"

♱ Cost of a Miracle ♱

A little girl went to her bedroom and removed a glass jar from a hiding place in the closet. She emptied the change on the bed and counted carefully. No room for error; the total had to be exact. Cautiously replacing the coins, she slipped out the back door and made her way to the drugstore. She waited patiently for the pharmacist to pay attention but he was too busy.

She scuffed her feet to make noise. She cleared her throat with the most disgusting sound she could muster. Finally, she took a quarter from her jar and etched it on the glass counter.

"What do you want?" the pharmacist asked angrily. "I'm talking to my brother whom I haven't seen in ages," he continued, not awaiting a reply.

She retorted, "I want to talk to you about my brother who's real sick. I need to buy a miracle."

"I beg your pardon?" exclaimed the pharmacist.

"He has something bad growing in his head and my Daddy says only a miracle can save him. So, how much does a miracle cost?"

"We don't sell miracles here, little girl. I'm sorry but I can't help you," the pharmacist replied, softening.

"I have money for it. If it isn't enough, I'll get the rest. Please, tell me how much it costs."

The pharmacist's well-dressed brother stooped and asked, "What kind of miracle does your brother need?"

"I don't know," she replied, her eyes welling up. "I just know he's real sick and Mommy says he needs an operation. But Daddy can't pay for it, so I want to use the money I saved."

"How much do you have?" asked the man.

"One dollar and eleven cents," she answered. "It's all I have, but I can get more if I need to."

He took the money and said, "What a coincidence, one dollar and eleven cents, precisely the cost of a miracle for little brothers."

The man, a surgeon specializing in neurosurgery, performed the operation successfully at no charge. Soon, her brother recovered.

Mommy and Daddy joyfully discussed the events. "The surgery was a real miracle. I wonder how much it cost."

Their daughter smiled for she knew exactly how much a miracle cost: one dollar and eleven cents plus the faith of a little child.

A miracle is not the suspension of natural law, but the operation of a higher law.

Jesus Saves

Jesus and Satan were arguing who was better on the computer. They had been at it for days and God was tired of the bickering. "I've had enough. I'm going to formulate a thorough two-hour test and from the results, I will judge the winner."

Satan and Jesus sat at their keyboards and typed away.

They moused.

They faxed.

They e-mailed.

They e-mailed with attachments.

They downloaded.

They did spreadsheets.

They wrote reports.

They created labels and cards.

They developed charts and graphs.

They researched genealogy reports.

They performed every job known to man.

Jesus worked with heavenly efficiency and Satan was faster than hell. Minutes prior to the bell, lightning flashed, thunder rolled, rain poured, and the power died.

Satan stared at his blank screen and cursed every swear word known in the underworld. Jesus sighed and sipped his Starbucks tazo chai latte.

Finally, electricity resumed and each rebooted his computer. Satan searched frantically, squealing, "I lost everything when the power went out."

Meanwhile, Jesus quietly printed his test results.

Satan became irate. "Wait," he screamed, "that's not fair. He cheated. How come he has all his work and I don't have any?"

God shrugged and said, "Jesus saves."

✝ Santa's Mom Clone ✝

'Twas the night before CHRISTmas, when all thru the abode,
Only one creature was stirring, she was cleaning the commode.
The children were finally sleeping, all snug in their beds,
Visions of Nintendo and Barbie flipping through their heads.

The dad was snoring in front of the TV
With a half-constructed bicycle propped on his knee.
So, only the mom heard the reindeer hooves clatter,
Which made her sigh, "Now, what's the matter?"

With toilet bowl brush still clutched in her hand,
She descended the stairs and saw the old man
Covered with ashes and soot, which fell with a shrug.
"Oh, great," muttered Mom, "Now I have to clean the rug."

"Ho, ho, ho," cried Santa, "I'm glad you're awake.
Your gift was especially difficult to make."
"Thanks, Santa, but all I want is some time alone."
"Exactly," he chuckled, "I've made you a clone."

"A clone?" she muttered. "What good is that?
Run along, Santa, I've no time for chitchat."
Then out walked the clone, the mother's twin,
Same hair, same eyes, same double chin.

"She'll cook, she'll dust, and she'll mop every mess.
You'll relax, take it easy, watch 'The Young and the Restless.'"
"Fantastic," the mom cheered. "My dream's come true.
I'll shop, I'll read, I'll sleep a night through."

From a room up above, the youngest did fret,
"Mommy, come quickly, I'm scared and I'm wet."

The clone replied, "I'm coming, sweetheart."
"Hey," the mom smiled, "She sure knows her part."

The clone changed the small one and hummed her a tune,
As she bundled the child in a warm blanket cocoon.
"You're the best mommy ever. I really love you."
The clone smiled and sighed, "And I love you, too."

The mom frowned and said, "Sorry, Santa, no deal.
That's my child's love she's trying to steal."
Grinning wisely, Santa said, "To me it is clear,
Only one loving mother is needed here."

The mom kissed her child and tucked her in bed.
"Thank you, Santa, for clearing my head.
I sometimes forget, it won't be very long,
When they'll be too old for my cradle and song."

The clock on the mantle began to chime.
Santa whispered to the clone, "It works every time."
With the clone by his side, Santa said, "Goodnight.
Merry CHRISTmas, dear Mom, you'll be all right."

✝ Are You Jesus? ✝

A group of salesmen attended an out-of-town convention. They had assured their wives they would be home for Friday's dinner. In the rush to their gate, one salesman inadvertently upset an apple display. Without stopping, they managed to reach their plane in time.

One salesman experienced a twinge of compassion for the operator of the apple cart. He told his friends to board without him and contact his wife on their arrival and explain his return on a later flight.

He rushed to the terminal where the apples indecorously dotted the tile floor. He was glad he did. The young girl who worked the apple counter was blind. With tears running down her cheeks, she was on the floor groping in frustration to recover her scattered fruit. No one in the crowd that swirled about had bothered to stop and help.

The salesman knelt beside her, gathered the apples in baskets, and helped rebuild the display. He noticed that many had been bruised and set them aside. When finished, he removed his wallet and offered, "Here, please take this money for the damage we did. Are you okay?"

She replied, "Yes," despite her tears.

He continued, "I hope we didn't spoil your day."

As he walked away, the bewildered blind girl cried out, "Mister?" He pivoted to gaze into those blind eyes. She queried, "Are you Jesus?"

He stopped in mid stride and pondered. Then he slowly made his way to the later flight with that question burning in his soul: *Are you Jesus*?

Do people mistake you for Jesus?

✟ Divine Windshield Wiper ✟

One rainy day, driving down the main street of town, I was taking the necessary precautions for slick, wet roads. Suddenly, my daughter Aspen spoke up from her relaxed position in her seat. "Dad, I'm thinking of something."

This announcement usually meant she had been pondering a while and was ready to expound what her six-year-old mind had discovered. "What are you thinking?" I asked eagerly.

She said, "The rain is like sin and the windshield wipers are like God wiping our sins away."

After the chill bumps raced up my arms, I was able to respond. "That's really good, Aspen." My curiosity grew. How far would my little girl take this revelation? I asked, "Do you notice how the rain keeps coming? What does that tell you?"

Aspen did not hesitate with her answer: "We keep on sinning and God keeps on forgiving."

I will always remember this when I turn on my wipers.

Spiritual Humor e-Soup — *A Compilation of Amusing Messages from the Internet*

Are You a Christian Impersonator?

A man was being tailgated by a woman and, suddenly, the traffic light turned yellow. He stopped even though he could have beaten the red by accelerating through the intersection.

The tailgating woman hit the horn and the brakes simultaneously. She screamed in frustration as she missed her chance to get through the intersection behind him. As she ranted, she heard a tap on her window and looked into the serious face of a police officer.

He ordered her to exit her car and escorted her to the station where she was searched, fingerprinted, photographed, and placed in a cell.

Hours later, a policeman escorted her from her cell to the booking desk where the arresting officer was waiting with her personal effects.

He offered, "I'm sorry for the mistake. You see, I pulled up behind you as you were blowing your horn at the car in front of you, hand-gesturing to the guy, and cussing a blue streak.

"I noticed the 'Choose Life' plate holder, the 'What Would Jesus Do' bumper sticker, the 'Follow Me to Sunday School' sticker, and the chrome-plated Christian fish emblem on the trunk.

"Naturally, I assumed you'd stolen the car."

If you were arrested and charged with being a Christian, could they find enough evidence to convict you?

⸭ Two Babes in a Manger ⸭

Two Americans answered an invitation to work in Russia. They taught in an orphanage for children who had been abandoned, abused, and left in the care of the government. They relate this story.

The holiday season offered an occasion for our orphans to hear the story of CHRISTmas for the first time. During the narration, they sat on the edges of their stools hanging on every word.

At the end, we helped them create their manger scenes from the scarce materials available. Each child had three pieces of cardboard to fashion a manger. They shredded yellow paper napkins and carefully laid the strips in the manger for straw. Small squares of flannel cut from a worn-out nightgown served as the baby's blanket. A doll-like baby was cut from tan felt we had brought from the United States.

The orphans were busy assembling their mangers as I circulated to see if they needed help. All went well until I arrived at Misha's table. He was about six years old and had finished his project. In his manger, I was startled to find not one, but two babies in the manger. I called for the translator to ask the youngster why there were two babies.

Crossing his arms and staring at his manger scene, the child very seriously repeated the story. For a young child, who had only heard the CHRISTmas story once, he related the events accurately until he came to where Mary placed Baby Jesus in the manger.

He ad-libbed the ending, "When Mary laid the baby in the manger, Jesus looked at me and asked if I had a place to stay. I told him I have no mamma and papa and no place to stay. Jesus told me I could stay with Him. I told Him I couldn't, because I didn't have a gift to give like everybody else.

"But I wanted so much to stay with Jesus. I thought about what I had that I could use for a gift and decided that if I kept Him warm, that would be a good gift.

"I asked, 'If I keep You warm, will that be a good enough gift?' Jesus said, 'Misha, if you keep Me warm, it would be the best gift anybody ever gave Me.'

"So, I crawled into the manger and Jesus told me I could stay with Him for always." Tears flooded his cheeks as he laid his head on the table and sobbed.

The little orphan found Someone who would never abandon or abuse him; Someone who would stay with him "for always."

Spiritual Humor e-Soup *A Compilation of Amusing Messages from the Internet*

What God Looks Like

A kindergarten teacher observed her classroom while they were drawing. She would stroll around to check each child's work. She asked one diligent little girl, "What are you drawing?"

The girl replied, "I'm drawing God."

The teacher paused and said, "But no one knows what God looks like."

Without missing a beat, the girl replied, "They will when I finish."

♰ Instructions for Life ♰

Great love and great achievements involve great risks.

When you lose, don't lose the lesson.

Follow the three Rs: respect for self, respect for others, and responsibility for all your actions.

Not getting what you want can be a fortuitous stroke of luck.

Don't be quick with the tongue; it cuts both ways.

Being kind is more important than being thought to be rich.

Don't let a little dispute injure a great relationship.

When you realize you have made a mistake, take immediate steps to correct it.

Spend some alone time every day.

Open arms to change but do not let go of your values.

Silence is sometimes the best answer.

Live a good, honorable life. When you get older and reminisce, you will be able to enjoy it a second time.

A loving atmosphere in your home is the foundation of your life.

In disagreements with loved ones, deal only with the current situation; do not bring up the past.

Share your knowledge; it is a way to achieve immortality.

Be gentle with the earth.

Once a year, go someplace you have never been.

The best relationship is one in which your love for each other exceeds your need for each other.

Judge your success by what you had to give up in order to get it.

Approach love and cooking with reckless abandon.

♰ Thank You to Our Military ♰

While flying on business, I noticed a Marine sergeant traveling with a folded flag, but failed to put two and two together. After boarding, I turned to the sergeant, who had been invited to sit in first class, and offered my hand, "Congratulations, young man, and thank you for your service to our country," and inquired, "Are you heading home?

"No, sir," he responded.

"Heading out?" I asked.

"No, sir, I'm escorting a soldier home," he replied.

"Going to pick him up?" I suggested densely.

"No, sir, he's with me. He was killed in Iraq and I'm taking him home to his family."

The realization of what he had been asked to do hit me like a ton of bricks. It was an honor for him, he confided. Although he did not know the soldier, he had delivered the news of his passing to his family and felt he knew them after many conversations.

I extended my hand again, "Thank you. Thank you for doing what you and your comrades do so my family and I can do what we do."

Upon landing, the pilot stopped short of the gate and announced, "Ladies and gentlemen, I would like to note that we've had the honor of Sergeant Steeley of the United States Marine Corps joining us. He is escorting a fallen comrade back home to his family. I ask that you please remain in your seats when we open the forward door to allow Sergeant Steeley to deplane and receive his fellow soldier. We will then turn off the seat belt sign."

Without a sound, all went as requested. I noticed the sergeant saluting the casket as it was brought off the plane. His action made me realize how proud I am to be an American.

Here is a public "Thank You" to our military men and women for what they do so we can live the way we do.

"Above all, we must realize that no arsenal, no weapon in the arsenals of the world, is so formidable as the will and moral courage of free men and women."

—Ronald Reagan, 40th President of the United States

Go to: www.yellowribbongreetings.us/farewellmarine.

Click on "Farewell Marine."

⌖ Spiritual First Aid Kit ⌖

Toothpick to remind you to pick out the good qualities in others.

Matthew 7:1

Rubber band to remind you to be flexible. Things might not always go the way you want, but it will work out.

Romans 8:28

Band-Aid to remind you to heal hurt feelings, yours or someone else's.

Colossians 3:12-14

Pencil to remind you to list your blessings every day.

Ephesians 1:3

Eraser to remind you that everyone makes mistakes, and it's okay.

Genesis 50:15-21

Chewing gum to remind you to stick with it and you can accomplish anything.

Philippians 4:13

Mint to remind you that you are worth a mint.

John 3:16-17

Tea bag to remind you to relax daily and review your list of blessings.

1 Thessalonians 5:18

✟ The W in CHRISTmas ✟

Each December, I vowed to make CHRISTmas a calm and peaceful experience. I had cut back on nonessential obligations: extensive card writing, endless baking, decorating, and, even, overspending. Yet, I found myself exhausted, unable to appreciate the precious family moments and, of course, the true meaning of CHRISTmas.

My son, Nicholas, was in kindergarten having an exciting time for a six-year-old. For weeks, he had been memorizing songs for his school's winter pageant.

I did not have the heart to tell him I would be working the night of the production. Unwilling to miss his shining moment, I spoke with his teacher and learned there would be a rehearsal the morning of the presentation. Parents unable to attend that evening were invited to come. Fortunately, my son seemed happy with the compromise.

That morning, I filed in ten minutes early, found a spot on the cafeteria floor, and sat down. Around the room, I noticed other parents quietly scampering to their seats. As we waited, the students filed in and each class, accompanied by their teacher, sat cross-legged on the floor. One by one, the groups rose to perform.

Since public schools had stopped referring to the holiday as "CHRISTmas," I did not expect anything other than fun, commercial entertainment: songs of reindeer, Santa Claus, snowflakes, and good cheer. So, when my son's class sang, "CHRISTmas Love," I was slightly taken aback by its bold acclamation.

Nicholas was aglow, as were his classmates, adorned in fuzzy mittens, red sweaters, and bright snow caps. Students in the front row held up posters to spell out the title of the song. As the class would sing, "C is for CHRISTmas," a child would raise the letter C. Then, "H is for Happy," and so on, until the children holding up their placards had spelled the complete message, "CHRISTmas Love."

The performance was going smoothly until a girl mistakenly held the letter M upside down, unaware her letter appeared as a W.

The audience of first through sixth graders snickered at this little one's error. She had no idea they were laughing at her, so she stood tall, proudly holding her W. Although teachers tried to quiet the children, commotion continued until the last letter was raised.

A hush came over the audience and eyes widened. Instantly, we understood the reason we were there, why we celebrated the holiday in the first place, why, even in the chaos, there was a purpose for our festivities. When the last letter was raised, the message proclaimed: CHRISTWASLOVE. And, I believe, He still is.

✟ Thank You for Friends ✟

Lord, thank You for loyal, loving friends
Who are there in winter, springtime, and fall.
New acquaintances are easy to come by,
But true friendship is extremely rare.

A friend always sees the best in you,
Although they've known you at your worst.
They laugh with you in the good times,
When storms threaten, they'll be there first.

They'll offer a shoulder to rest your head
When tears are welling in your eyes;
Take a walk down friendship's path with you
And help chase away those stormy skies.

Lord, thank You for all the gifts You give.
Each one makes our life seem more worthwhile.
But one of the finest gifts you've given us
Is the warmth of friendship's loving smile.

✟ Around the Corner I Have a Friend ✟

Around the corner I have a friend,
In this great city that has no end.
Yet the days go by and weeks rush on,
And before I know it, a year is gone.

And I never see my old friend's face,
For life is a swift and terrible race.
He knows I like him just as well,
As in the days when I rang his bell

And he rang mine. But we were younger then,
And now we are busy, tired men.
Tired of playing a foolish game,
Tired of trying to make a name.

"Tomorrow," I say, "I will call on Jim,
Just to show that I'm thinking of him."
But tomorrow comes and tomorrow goes,
And distance between us grows and grows.

Around the corner, yet miles away,
"Here's a telegram, sir, Jim died today."
And that's what we get and deserve in the end,
Around the corner, a vanished friend.

✝ Since Evil Exists, God Is Evil ✝

The university professor challenged his students, "Did God create everything that exists?"

A student bravely replied, "Yes, he did."

"God created everything?" the professor asked.

"Yes, sir," the student repeated, Adam's apple rippling in his throat.

The professor answered, "If God created everything, then God created evil. Since evil exists, according to the principle that our works define who we are, then God is evil."

The students were quieted by his pronouncement. The professor, pleased with himself, boasted that he had proven once more that the Christian faith was a myth.

A student raised his hand and asked, "Can I ask you a question?"

"Of course," replied the preening professor.

The student stood and posed, "Professor, does cold exist?"

"What kind of question is that? Of course, it exists. Have you never been cold?" The class snickered at the young man's question.

He stated, "In fact, sir, cold does not exist. According to the laws of physics, what we consider cold is in reality the absence of heat. Every body or object is susceptible to study when it has or transmits energy, and heat is what makes a body or matter have or transmit energy.

"Absolute zero, minus 460 degrees Fahrenheit, is the total absence of heat; all matter becomes inert and incapable of reaction at that temperature. Cold does not exist. We have created this word to describe how we feel if we have no heat."

The student continued, "Professor, does darkness exist?"

The professor responded, "Of course, it does."

The student replied, "Once again you are wrong. Darkness does not exist either. Darkness is in reality the absence of light. Light we can study, but not darkness. In fact, we can use Newton's prism to break white light into many colors and study the various wavelengths of each color. You cannot measure darkness. A simple ray of light can break into a world of darkness and illuminate it.

"How can you know how dark a certain space is? You measure the amount of light present. Darkness is a term used by man to describe what happens when there is no light present."

The young man challenged, "Professor, does evil exist?"

Less stridently, he replied, "As I proved, we see it every day in the form of man's inhumanity to man, in the crime and violence everywhere. These manifestations are nothing but evil."

The student retorted, "Evil does not exist, sir, or, at least, it does not exist unto itself. Evil is simply the absence of God; like darkness and cold, a word that man has created to describe the absence of God.

"God did not create evil. Evil is not like faith or love that exist as do light and heat. Evil is the result of what happens when man does not have God's love present in his heart. It is like the cold that comes when there is no heat or the darkness that comes when there is no light."

The professor sat down, quieted.

Spiritual Humor e-Soup — *A Compilation of Amusing Messages from the Internet*

God Was Busy

A college professor, an avowed atheist, shocked his class by declaring he was going to prove there was no God. Addressing the ceiling, he shouted, "God, if you're real, I want you to knock me off this platform within the next fifteen minutes."

The room fell silent. Ten minutes passed and he taunted, "Here I am, God. I'm still waiting."

His countdown neared the last minutes when a Marine, recently released from active duty, strolled up to the professor, punched him in the face, and sent him tumbling from his platform. The professor was out cold.

The students were shocked and babbled in confusion. The young Marine took a seat in the front row and sat silent. The class fell silent and waited.

Eventually, the professor came to, still shaken, and glared at the Marine. When he regained his senses, he demanded, "What's the matter with you? Why'd you do that?"

"God was busy. He called in the Marines."

✝ Résumé of Jesus Christ ✝

Address: Ephesians 1:20

Phone: Romans 10:13

Website: The Bible

Keywords: Christ, Lord, Savior, and Jesus

My name is Jesus, the Christ; called Lord by many. I have sent my résumé because I am seeking the top management position in your heart. Please consider my accomplishments as set forth.

Qualifications:

I founded the earth and established the heavens. Proverbs 3:19

I formed man from the dust of the ground. Genesis 2:7

I breathed into man the breath of life. Genesis 2:7

I redeemed man from the curse of the law. Galatians 3:13

The blessings of the Abrahamic Covenant come upon your life through me. Galatians 3:14

Occupational Background:

I have had only one employer. Luke 2:49

I have never been tardy, absent, disobedient, slothful, or disrespectful. My employer has nothing but rave reviews for me. Matthew 3:15-17

Skills and Work Experiences:

Empowering the poor to be poor no more, healing the brokenhearted, setting the captives free, healing the sick, restoring sight to the blind, and setting at liberty them that are bruised. Luke 4:18

I am a wonderful Counselor. Isaiah 9:6

People who listen to me shall dwell safely and not fear evil. Proverbs 1:33

I have the authority, ability, and power to cleanse you of your sins. I John 1:7-9

Educational Background:

I encompass the entire breadth and length of knowledge, wisdom, and understanding. Proverbs 2:6

In me are hid all of the treasures of wisdom and knowledge. Colossians 2:3

My Word is so powerful, it has been described as being a lamp unto your feet and unto your path. Psalms 119:105

I can tell you all the secrets of your heart. Psalms 44:21

Major Accomplishments:
I was an active participant in the greatest summit meeting of all times. Genesis 1:26

I laid down my life so that you may live. 2 Corinthians 5:15

I defeated the arch enemy of God and mankind and made a show of them openly. Colossians 2:15

I have miraculously fed the poor, healed the sick, and raised the dead. There are many more, too many to mention here. You can read them on my website; you do not need an Internet connection or computer to access www.thebible.god

References:
Believers and followers worldwide will testify to my divine healings, salvation, deliverance, miracles, restoration, and supernatural guidance.

In Summation:
I am confident I am the only candidate uniquely qualified to fill this vital position in your heart.

I will properly direct your paths. Proverbs 3:5-6

I will lead you into everlasting life. John 6:47

When can I start? Time is of the essence. Hebrews 3:15

✟ How to Reduce Stress ✟

1. Pray.
2. Go to bed on time.
3. Get up on time so you can start the day unrushed.
4. Say "no" to projects that will not fit into your schedule or that will compromise your mental health.
5. Delegate tasks to capable others.

6. Simplify and un-clutter your life.
7. Less is more. If one is often not enough, two are often too many.
8. Allow extra time to do things and to get to places.
9. Pace yourself. Spread out big changes and difficult projects over time. Do not lump the hard things all together.
10. Take one day at a time.
11. Separate worries from concerns. If a situation is a concern, find out what God would have you to do and let go of the anxiety. If you cannot do anything about a situation, forget it.
12. Live within your budget.
13. Have backups: extra car key in your wallet, extra house key buried in the garden, extra stamps, and so on.
14. KYMS - Keep Your Mouth Shut. This single piece of advice can prevent an enormous amount of trouble.
15. Do something for the kid in you regularly.
16. Carry a Bible with you to read while waiting in line.
17. Eat right and exercise.
18. Get organized so everything has its place.
19. In the car, listen to a tape that can improve your quality of life.
20. Write thoughts and inspirations down.
21. Every day, find time to be alone.
22. Having problems? Talk to God on the spot. Nip small problems in the bud. Do not wait until it is bedtime to pray.
23. Make friends with godly people.
24. Keep a folder of favorite scriptures on hand.
25. Remember that the shortest bridge between despair and hope is often a heartfelt "Thank you, Jesus."

26. Laugh loud and often.

27. Laugh some more.

28. Take your work seriously, but yourself not at all.

29. Develop a forgiving attitude. People are doing the best they can.

30. Be kind to unkind people. They probably need it the most.

31. Sit on your ego.

32. Talk less; listen more.

33. Slow down.

34. Remember that you are not the general manager of the universe.

35. Every night before bed, think of one thing you are grateful for that you have never been grateful for before.

36. Have faith that God has a way of turning things around for you.

A Reason, a Season, or a Lifetime

People come into your life for a reason, a season, or a lifetime. When you discern which, you will know what to do for that person.

When someone is in your life for a reason, it is usually to meet a need you have expressed. They have come to assist you through a difficulty, to provide you with guidance and support, or to aid you physically, emotionally, or spiritually. They may seem like a godsend and they are. They are there for the reason you need them to be.

Then, without any wrongdoing on your part or at an inconvenient time, this person will say or do something to bring the relationship to an end. They die, walk away, act up, and force you to take a stand. What we must realize is that our need has been met, our desire fulfilled, their work done. Your prayer has been answered and it is time to move on.

Some people come into your life for a season because your turn has come to share, grow, or learn. They bring peace or make you laugh. They may teach you something you never knew. They usually give you an unbelievable amount of joy. Believe it, it is real; but only for a season.

Lifetime relationships teach you lifetime lessons, things you must build upon in order to have a solid foundation. Your job is to accept the lesson, love the person, and put what you have learned to use in your life.

Thank you for being part of my life, whether you were a reason, a season, or a lifetime.

✟ Precious Gifts from the Heart ✟

Lord, I wish for roses, perfuming my day.
For walking a petal-strewn path would be a happy way.
But I find I don't have all I wish; at least not yet, awhile.
Would You be desiring something better, found through a deeper trial?

Do You keep me from knowing all, for too much I'm unable to contain?
Are You showing me there's greater joy in learning faith through pain?
Are You letting me know a darkness so I will seek Your light;
To search until I find You, the door to escape the gloom of night?

Will you allow me these limitations so I can learn the more,
Just as a jewel will shine when tumbled to remove a flaw?
In new challenges that descend, shall I find You are true?
Will I learn, then, how to trust Your love, rather than all I can
and cannot do?

Would You let me struggle to find the answers You can give?
And, if I ask, will You bestow the wisdom I will need to live?
For, if things don't come my way, will I learn a grateful heart;
To enter into a real joy, for contentment that will not part?

Is this key of gratitude what turns the bad things into good?
So that troubles become a blessing; to grow just as I should?
For, life is such a journey where I may feel betrayed.
But, what understanding will I learn for others crying in the shade?

If it weren't for the times I learn my God is near,
I wouldn't know where to find the strength to persevere.
For, everything I cannot know gives me so much to learn
And all I don't have yet, become an expectant hope to yearn.

So, take me on Your path, dear Lord, with Your roses, all the way.
Shower me with the loving gifts that You have planned today.
Give me, from Your heart of love, all that You say to give away.
But I thank You for the heartaches, Lord, that really are Your bouquet.

✝ Heaven's Grocery Store ✝

Stumbling down life's highway, I came upon a sign that read Heaven's Grocery Store. As I approached, doors swung open. On entering, a host of angels greeted me. One handed me a basket and said, "My child, shop with care." Everything a human needed was stocked on the shelves. So, I shopped until I dropped:

First I got some Patience. Love was in the same row.
Further on was Understanding; you need that everywhere you go.
I got a box or two of Wisdom, and Faith a bag or two.
And Charity, of course, I would need some of that too.

I couldn't miss the Holy Spirit; He was all over the place.
Then some Strength and Courage to help me run this race.
And then I chose Salvation for it was for free.
I tried to get enough to do for you and for me.

Then I started to the counter to pay my grocery bill,
For I thought I had everything to do the Master's will.
As I went up the aisle, I saw Prayer and put that in,
For I knew when I stepped outside I would run into sin.

Peace and Joy were plentiful, the last things on the shelf.
Song and Praise were hanging near so I just helped myself.
My basket was getting full but I remembered I needed Grace,
Fortunately for me, God placed it directly in front of my face.

Then I said to the angel, "How much do I owe?"
He smiled and said, "Just take them everywhere you go."
Again I asked, "Really, how much do I owe?"
"My child," he said, "Jesus paid your bill a long time ago."

✟ Mousetrap ✟

A mouse peeking through a crack in the wall saw the farmer and his wife open a package. He thought, *What food might this contain*? but was shocked to learn it was a mousetrap. Retreating to the farmyard, he cried, "There's a mousetrap in the house; there's a mousetrap in the house."

The chicken raised her head to cluck, "Mr. Mouse, I can tell this is of grave concern to you, but of no consequence to me. I cannot be bothered by it."

The mouse turned to the pig, "There is a mousetrap in the house."

The pig sympathized, "I am so very sorry, Mr. Mouse, but there is nothing I can do about it but pray. Be assured that you are in my prayers."

The mouse turned to the cow. She said, "Mr. Mouse, I'm sorry for you. But it's no skin off my nose." The dejected mouse retreated to the house to face the mousetrap alone.

That night, a sound of a mousetrap catching its prey rippled throughout the house. The wife rushed to see what was caught. In the darkness, she did not see that it was a venomous snake whose tail the trap had grabbed. The snake bit her and the farmer rushed her to the hospital. She returned home with a fever.

Everyone knows you treat a fever with fresh chicken soup, so the farmer took his hatchet to the farmyard for the soup's main ingredient. His wife's illness continued, so friends and neighbors came to sit with her around the clock. To feed them, the farmer butchered the pig.

The wife did not recover and died. Many people attended her funeral and the farmer had the cow slaughtered to provide enough meat for them.

✝ The Tablecloth ✝

The new pastor and his wife arrived in Brooklyn in early October thrilled about their assignment to reopen a church. Their church was run down and needed much work. They set a goal to complete the renovation in time to hold their first service on CHRISTmas Eve.

They worked hard repairing pews, plastering walls, and painting, and on December 18 were almost finished. But on December 19, a terrible two-day tempest hit the area.

On the twenty-first, the pastor checked the church and his heart sank when he learned the roof had leaked. A large area of wall behind the pulpit about head high had split open. He cleaned the mess and, not knowing what else to do, canceled the CHRISTmas Eve service and headed home.

On the way, he noticed a thrift shop having a sale and stopped in. One item was a handmade tablecloth with exquisite crochet work, fine colors, and a cross embroidered in the center. It was the right size to cover the hole in the wall. He bought it and returned to the church.

By this time, it had started to snow. An older woman running from the opposite direction was trying to catch the bus but missed it. The pastor invited her to wait in the church for the next bus.

She sat in a pew and paid no attention while he got a ladder to hang the tablecloth as a wall tapestry. He could hardly believe how beautiful it looked as it covered the damaged area.

The woman approached from the back pew. Her face white as a sheet, she gasped, "Pastor, where did you find that tablecloth?"

He explained and she asked him to check the lower right corner for the initials EBG. He found them. They were hers: She had made the tablecloth thirty-five years earlier in Austria.

The woman said that before the war she and her husband were citizens of Austria. When the Nazis arrived, she was forced to leave. Her husband was going to follow but was captured, sent to prison, and never seen again.

The pastor wanted to give her the tablecloth, but she insisted he keep it for the church. The pastor offered to drive her home, the least he could do. She lived on Staten Island and was in Brooklyn for the day for a doctor's appointment.

What a wonderful CHRISTmas Eve they celebrated. The church was full and the music and spirit were lively. At the end, the pastor and his wife met everyone at the door and many said they would return. An older man, whom the pastor knew from the neighborhood, continued to sit in the pew and stare ahead. The pastor asked, "Can I help you with anything?"

The man asked where he got the tablecloth. It was identical to one his wife made when they lived in Austria before the war. He told the pastor when the Nazis came he forced his wife to flee for her safety. He was supposed to follow, but was arrested and put in a prison. He never saw his wife again.

The pastor asked if he would come with him for a ride. They drove to the house where the pastor had taken the woman. He helped the man climb the three flights to the apartment, knocked on the door, and witnessed the greatest CHRISTmas reunion he could ever imagine.

✢ Our Quilt of Life ✢

As I faced my Maker at the last judgment, I knelt before Him with the other souls. In front of us laid our lives in piles of square fabric like a quilt. An angel sat before us sewing our squares into a tapestry that represented our life.

As my angel sewed my squares, I noticed they were ragged and contained large holes. Each piece was labeled with a portion of my life; challenges and temptations I faced. Hardships that I endured made the largest holes.

I glanced around and nobody else had such squares. Other than a tiny hole here and there, the other tapestries held rich color and bright hues of worldly fortune. I gazed sadly upon my tapestry. Sewing together the threadbare, tattered pieces of my life was like binding air.

The time came when each life was to be displayed; held up to the light, the scrutiny of truth. Each soul rose in turn, presenting their tapestry; so rich their lives had been.

My angel signaled my turn. My eyes dropped to the ground in shame. I had not had the earthly fortunes. I had love and laughter in my life but there had also been trials of illness, death, and false accusations that took me from my life as I knew it.

I had to start over many times and struggled with the temptation to quit. Somehow I mustered the strength to go on. I spent many nights in prayer. I had been unfairly ridiculed and endured it by offering it up to the Father in hopes I would not fall.

Presently, I had to face the truth. My life was what it was and I had to accept it. I rose and lifted the combined squares of my life to the light. An awe-filled gasp split the air and the others gaped at me. I stared at the tapestry before me. Light flooded the holes creating an image, the face of Christ.

Then, our Lord appeared before me and said, "Each time you gave your life to Me, it became My life, My hardships, and My struggles. Each ray of light in your life is when you stepped aside and let Me shine through until there was more of Me than there was of you."

May your quilt be threadbare and worn, allowing Christ to shine through.

✥ What Heaven Was Like ✥

Brian Moore had a short time to write a paper on What Heaven Was Like. He told his father, Bruce, "It's the best thing I ever wrote." It was also the last. Brian died when his car went off the road and struck a utility pole. He emerged unharmed but stepped on a downed power line and was electrocuted.

His parents framed Brian's essay and hung it among the family portraits. "I think God used Brian to make a point and we were meant to make something of it," Mrs. Moore said of the essay. She and her husband want to share their son's vision of life after death. "I'm happy for Brian. I know he's in heaven. I know I'll see him. Here's his essay:"

In that vague space between wakefulness and sleep, I dreamed I found myself in a room with no distinguishing features except a wall covered with files. They looked like library indexes that list authors, titles, or subject in alphabetical order. But these files, stretching from floor to ceiling, endlessly in either direction, had very different headings.

As I drew near, the first to catch my attention read *Girls I liked.* I opened it and flipped through the cards but shut it quickly when I realized I recognized the names. Without being told, I knew precisely where I was.

This limitless room of countless cards was a system cataloging my life. The cards recorded accounts of my every moment, in detail my memory could not match. A feeling of wonder and curiosity, coupled with horror, stirred in me as I randomly explored the contents. Some brought joy and sweet memories; others, a sense of shame and regret so intense I peeked over my shoulder to make sure nobody was watching.

A file *Friends* abutted one marked *Friends I betrayed.* Titles ranged from the mundane to outright weird: *Books I read, Lies I told, Comfort I gave, Jokes I laughed at.* Some were hilarious in their exactness: *Things I yelled at my brothers*. Others, I could not laugh at: *Things I did in anger, Things I muttered under my breath at my parents*. The range of topics never ceased to surprise me.

Too often, there were more cards than I expected and, at times, fewer than hoped. The sheer volume of my activities overwhelmed me. Was it possible I had the time in my short span to produce these thousands, perhaps millions of cards? Every card confirmed the truth as they were written in my handwriting and sealed by my signature.

When I removed *TV shows I watched*, I noticed the file depth grew in relation to the number of events. The cards were tightly packed but after six feet I had not sighted the light at the end. I shut the drawer in shame, not so much by the quality of TV shows, more by the amount of wasted time the file represented.

When I came to *Lustful thoughts,* a chill raced through my body. I pulled out the file an inch, unwilling to test its depth, and withdrew a card. I shuddered at the detail. Sick to think that such moments had been recorded, one thought dominated: *I have to destroy these cards*.

In an insane frenzy, I yanked the file out. The depth did not matter. I had to empty it and burn the evidence. I grabbed an end and banged it on the floor but could not dislodge a single card. Desperate, I tried to rip out a card only to find it as strong as steel.

Utterly defeated, I replaced the file. Leaning my head against the cabinets, I gasped a long, self-pitying sigh. Then I saw it, *People I shared the gospel with*. The handle was brighter than the others, newer, almost unused. I jerked the shiny handle and stumbled off balance as a short file fell into my lap. I could count the cards on one hand.

Tears slowly turned to rivulets. Sobs followed; sobs so deep they racked my body. I fell to my knees and cried from the overwhelming shame. The rows and rows of files swirled in my tear-clouded eyes. No one must ever learn of this room. I must lock it and destroy the key.

I arose to effect my plan when I saw Him. No, please, not Him. Not here. Oh, anyone but Jesus. I watched powerlessly as He opened the files and read the cards. I could not bear to witness His reaction but I could not take my eyes from Him. When I gazed upon His face, I saw a sorrow and anguish deeper than my own.

Intuitively, He began with the worst files and read every card. Finally, He gazed upon me, not in pity, but with mercy. I collapsed on the floor, covered my head with my arms, and wept. He walked over, knelt, and embraced me. He could have said so many things but He did not utter a word. He cried with me.

After consoling me, He went to the wall, removed files, one by one, and inscribed His name on the cards. I shouted, "No!" and yanked the file from Him. "Your name doesn't belong on these." But it was, His name written in His blood concealed mine.

He smiled and continued to sign the cards. I will never understand how He finished so quickly. He closed the last file and returned to me. He placed His hand on my forehead and said, "It is finished," and led me out of the room.

What is the depth of your People I Shared the Gospel With *file?*

☩ An Obituary, Jerusalem, 33 A.D. ☩

Jesus Christ, 33, of Nazareth, died Friday on Mount Calvary, also known as Golgotha, "the place of the skull." Betrayed by the apostle Judas, He was crucified by order of ruler Pontius Pilate. The causes of death were asphyxiation by crucifixion, extreme exhaustion, severe torture, and loss of blood.

Jesus Christ, descendant of Abraham, was a member of the house of David. He was Son of the late Joseph, a carpenter of Nazareth, and Mary, His devoted Mother. Jesus was born in a stable in the city of Bethlehem, Judea. He is survived by His mother Mary, His faithful Apostles, numerous disciples, and many followers.

Jesus was self-educated and spent most of His adult life working as a teacher. Jesus occasionally worked as a medical doctor and it is reported that He healed many patients. Until the time of His death, He was sharing the Good News by healing the sick, touching the lonely, feeding the hungry, and helping the poor.

Jesus was most noted for recounting parables about His Father's Kingdom, performing miracles, such as feeding more than five thousand people with only five loaves of bread and two fish, and healing a man born blind. The day before His death, He held a last supper celebrating the Passover feast at which He foretold His death.

The body was buried in a grave donated by Joseph of Arimathea, a family friend. By order of Pontius Pilate, a boulder was rolled in front of the tomb and Roman soldiers were stationed on guard.

In lieu of flowers, the family has requested that everyone try to live as Jesus did. Donations may be sent to anyone in need.

✞ A Dog's Best Friend ✞

A man and his dog were walking along a road. The man was enjoying the scenery when it occurred to him that he was dead. He remembered dying, and the dog walking beside him had been dead for years. He wondered where the road was leading.

After a ways, they came to a fine, white marble wall alongside the road. Ahead, atop a hill, it was breached by an arch that glowed with sunlight. Nearing it, he saw a magnificent gate that appeared to be mother-of-pearl and a street that led to the gate looked like pure gold.

He and the dog walked to the gate and he noticed a man at a desk to one side. He called out, "Excuse me, where are we?"

"This is Heaven, sir," the man answered.

"Wow. Would you happen to have some water?" the man asked.

"Of course, sir, come right in and I'll have ice water brought right away." The man gestured and the gate swung wide.

"Can my friend," nodding to his dog, "come in, too?" he asked.

"I'm sorry, sir, but we don't accept pets."

The man thought a second, returned to the road, and continued on his way. After another trek, atop another hill, he came to a dirt road, which led through a gate that looked like it had never been closed. There was no fence. As he neared the gate, he noticed a man leaning against a tree reading a book.

"Excuse me," he called to the reader. "Do you have any water?"

"Yeah, sure, there's a pump over there. Come on in."

"How about my friend here?" the traveler pointed to the dog.

"Should be a bowl by the pump," he said assuredly.

They entered and, sure enough, there was an old-fashioned hand pump with a bowl beside it. He filled the bowl for his dog and took a long swig direct from the pump. After, he and the dog walked toward the man standing by the tree.

"What do you call this place?" the traveler asked.

"This is Heaven," he answered.

"Well, that's confusing," the traveler said. "The man down the road said that was Heaven."

"Oh, you mean the place with the gold streets and pearly gates? Nope. That's Hell," he replied.

"Doesn't it make you mad for them to use your name like that?" asked the traveler.

"No, we're happy they screen out the folks who would leave their best friends behind."

✟ Directions to Our Father's House ✟

Make a right turn onto Believeth Boulevard.

Keep straight and go through the green light that is Jesus Christ.

Turn onto the Bridge of Faith over troubled water.

When you get off the bridge, make a right turn and keep straight.

You are on King's Highway, Heaven-bound.

Keep going for three miles: One for the Father, One for the Son, and One for the Holy Spirit.

Exit onto Grace Boulevard and make a right turn on Gospel Lane.

Keep straight and make another right on Prayer Road.

On your way, yield not to the traffic on Temptation Avenue.

Also, avoid Sin Street because it is a dead end.

Quickly pass Envy Drive and Hate Avenue.

Also, pass Hypocrisy Street, Gossiping Lane, and Backbiting Boulevard.

However, you have to go down Long-suffering Lane, Persecution Boulevard, as well as Trials and Tribulations Avenue.

But that is all right, because Victory Lane to our Father's house is straight ahead.

✟ Searching for CHRISTmas ✟

One CHRISTmas night, Our Lord came down into a modern city to see what people were doing. Everyone was celebrating Happy Holidays. Christ met a policeman directing traffic and asked, "What does 'Happy Holidays' mean?"

The policeman eyed Him suspiciously. "Where are you from?"

"Bethlehem," Christ replied.

"Where?" badgered the officer.

"Bethlehem," Our Lord repeated.

"Don't you know it's a holiday for kids?" the policeman sputtered.

"What is the origin of the holiday?" Our Lord asked.

"Look, you ask too many questions. Can't you see I'm busy?" blurted the policeman.

Next, Christ paused by a restaurant advertising "CHRISTmas Party-$50." Ladies and gentlemen in elegant attire were entering. He stepped inside. Tables elegantly covered with white linen and CHRISTmas candles were arranged in rows. A woman, eyeing Our Lord, complained loudly, "You let beggars in here!"

The waiter rushed over and demanded, "What are you doing in here? Go beg on the street."

Christ studied the young man. "If you only knew what I am 'begging' for," He started to reply before being evicted, as the woman playing the piano sang, "Peace on earth and mercy mild."

Outside, Christ allowed Himself to be swept along by the throng that flowed like a river between stores. He saw toys everywhere, but rarely a Nativity scene. He found Himself near a school playground. Above the gate was a sign: "CHRISTmas Party for Children."

Our Lord went inside and witnessed hundreds of children receiving toys. As they noisily ran and tumbled, important-looking women hurried about. Neither a Nativity scene nor a crucifix could be seen. Nobody mentioned the Child Jesus. As Christ stood there, a feeling of isolation grew in His heart. He felt like a trespasser. He approached a young boy whose arms overflowed with toys. "Do you love the Child Jesus who gave you so many nice toys?" Our Lord asked.

The boy stared at Him, puzzled, "What Child Jesus?"

"Don't you know Him?" repeated Christ.

"No," answered the boy.

The school headmaster rushed over. "What did this man say to you?" she frantically asked the boy. Learning what Our Lord had asked and Whose Name He had dared mention, her eyes glared and she snarled, "You need to leave — now!"

Christ left and continued to walk through the streets, passing innumerable places where His creatures celebrated CHRISTmas without knowing why. Weary, He came to a neglected suburb. A building with tiny lights caught His eye. Approaching a window, He saw His image displayed on the wall. His eyes brightened when He noticed a simple but attractively arranged crèche. Just then, the door opened and a boy came out. The boy stopped abruptly at the sight of the man shivering in the darkness. Icy gusts blew around them. "Sir, you could freeze out here. You need to get out of the cold."

"I am quite cold," answered Our Lord.

"Come in, then. We have a good fire going."

Our Lord entered. Near the fireplace, children gathered around a young priest. As the fire crackled, the priest told the children about the infinite grandeur and glory hidden within the little figure of the Child Jesus. He paused the moment Our Lord entered. "Come in. You look cold. Please, warm yourself here." The children promptly offered the newcomer a place close to the fire.

"Have you had anything to eat? Joseph, go ask your mother to prepare something hot for this gentleman." Christ's gaze rested on them, one by one, as if He were memorizing every little face. Above all, He gazed at the young priest. "Are you alone, my friend?" asked the priest kindly.

"Yes." All eyes turned curiously on the Stranger, waiting. Christ did not speak. Very slowly, regally, Jesus' hand moved. He extended it over their heads, as if reaching beyond the humble cottages of that poor suburb, and encompassing the city whose miseries He had witnessed, He exclaimed, "Misereor super turbas!" (I have pity on these people!). Then, slowly, before their astonished eyes, He disappeared.

"It was He!" cried one of the boys.

The priest nodded solemnly. "Yes, it was."

Reprinted with the permission of Tradition Family Property Student Action.
Visit their website at www.tfp.org/sa

⚜ I Wish You Enough ⚜

I overheard a mother and daughter in their last moments together at the airport. Standing near the security gate, they hugged and the mother said, "I love you and I wish you enough."

The daughter replied, "Mom, our life together has been more than enough. Your love is all I needed. I wish you enough, too."

They kissed and the daughter left. The mother walked over to the window where I was seated. I could tell she wanted and needed to cry. I tried not to intrude but she welcomed me in by asking, "Did you ever say good-bye to someone knowing it would be forever?"

"Yes, I have," I replied. "Forgive me for prying, but why is this a 'forever' good-bye?"

"I am old and she lives so far away. I have challenges ahead and the reality is her next trip back will be for my funeral," she said.

"When you were saying good-bye, I heard you say, 'I wish you enough.' May I ask what that means?"

She smiled. "That's a wish that has been handed down from other generations. My parents used to say it to everyone."

She paused and looked up as if trying to remember it in detail and, smiling wider, stated, "When we said, 'I wish you enough,' we were wanting the other person to have a life filled with enough good things to sustain them."

Turning to me, she shared by reciting from memory:

"I wish you enough sun to keep your attitude bright.

I wish you enough rain to appreciate the sun more.

I wish you enough happiness to keep your spirit alive.

I wish you enough pain so the smallest joys in life appear much bigger.

I wish you enough gain to satisfy your wanting.

I wish you enough loss to appreciate what you possess.

I wish you enough hellos to get you through the final good-bye."

She began to cry and walked away.

✟ God's Spider ✟

During World War II on a Pacific island, a U.S. marine was separated from his unit. The fighting had been intense, and in the smoke and crossfire he had lost touch with his comrades.

Alone in the jungle, he could hear enemy soldiers coming in his direction. Scrambling for cover, he found his way up a high ridge to several small caves in the rock. Quickly he crawled inside. Although safe for the moment, he realized that once the enemy swept up the ridge, they would search the caves and he would be killed.

As he waited, he prayed, "Lord, if it be Your will, please, protect me. Whatever Your will though, I love You and trust You. Amen."

After praying, he lay quietly, listening to the enemy begin to draw close. He thought, Well, I guess the Lord isn't going to help me out of this one. Then he saw a spider begin to build a web over the front of his cave.

As he watched, listening to the enemy search for him, the spider layered strand after strand of web across the cave opening. Hah, he thought. What I need is a brick wall and what the Lord has sent me is a spider web. God does have a sense of humor.

He watched from the darkness of his hideout as the enemy searched one cave after another. As they neared his, he readied to make his last stand. To his amazement, however, after glancing in the direction of his cave, they moved on.

He realized that with the spider web over the entrance, his cave looked as if no one had entered for quite a while. "Lord, forgive me," prayed the young man. "I had forgotten that in You a spider's web is stronger than a brick wall."

✟ Explanation of the Existence of God ✟

A man went to a barbershop to have his hair cut and beard trimmed. As the barber began to work, they started up a conversation on many topics.

When they eventually touched on the subject of God, the barber said, "I don't believe that God exists."

"Why do you say that?" asked the customer.

"Well, you only need to go out in the street to realize God doesn't exist. Tell me, if God exists, would there be so many sick people? Would there be abandoned children? If God existed, there would be neither suffering nor pain. I can't imagine a loving God who would allow it."

The customer did not respond because he did not want to start an argument. The barber finished his job and the customer left. Soon after he left the barbershop, the customer saw an unkempt man in the street with long, stringy, dirty hair and an untrimmed beard.

The customer returned to the barber shop and said to the barber, "You know what? Barbers do not exist."

"How can you say that?" asked the surprised barber. "I am here, and I am a barber. And I worked on you."

"No," the customer exclaimed. "Barbers don't exist because if they did, there would be no people with dirty long hair and untrimmed beards, like that man outside."

"Ah, but barbers do exist. What happens is, people do not come to me."

"Exactly," affirmed the customer. "That's the point. God, too, does exist. What happens is, people don't go to Him and that's why there's so much pain and suffering in the world."

✟ I Chose to Live ✟

John is the kind of guy you love to hate: always in a good mood and something positive to say. When someone asks, "How are you?" he replies, "If I were any better, I'd be twins."

He was a natural motivator. If an employee was having a bad day, John was there telling the employee how to look on the positive side of the situation.

His style made me curious, so one day I asked, "I don't get it, John. You can't be positive all the time. How do you do it?"

He said, "Each morning I wake up and say to myself, 'You have two choices today. You can choose to be in a good mood or to be in a bad mood.' I choose to be in a good mood."

"Each time something bad happens, I can choose to be a victim or to learn from it. I choose to learn from it.

"Every time someone comes to me complaining, I can choose to accept their complaining or I can point out the positive side of life. I choose the positive side of life."

"Yeah, right, it's not that easy," I protested.

"Yes, it is," he said. "Life is about choices. When you cut away the junk, every situation is a choice. You choose how you react to situations. You choose how people affect your mood. You choose to be in a good mood or bad mood. The bottom line: It's your choice how you live your life."

I reflected on his philosophy. Soon after, I left to start my business. We lost touch, but I often thought about him when I made a choice about life instead of reacting to it.

Years later, I heard he was involved in a serious accident, falling sixty feet from a tower. After eighteen hours of surgery to place rods in his back and weeks of intensive care, he was released from the hospital.

I saw him about six months later. When I asked how he was, he replied, "If I were any better, I'd be twins. Wanna see my scars?"

I declined the offer but did ask him what had gone through his mind as the accident took place.

"The first thing was the well-being of my soon-to-be born child. Then, as I lay on the ground, I remembered I had two choices: I could choose to live or to die. I chose to live."

"Weren't you scared? Did you lose consciousness?" I asked.

He continued, "The paramedics were great. They kept telling me I was going to be fine. But when they wheeled me into the emergency room, I saw the expressions on the faces of the doctors and nurses and got scared. In their eyes, I read, 'He's a dead man.' I knew I needed to take action."

"What did you do?" I asked.

"Well, there was a big burly nurse shouting questions at me. She asked if I was allergic to anything. 'Yes,' I replied. The doctors and nurses stopped working as they awaited my reply. I took a deep breath and yelled, 'Gravity.'

"Over their laughter, I told them, 'I'm choosing to live. Operate on me as if I'm alive, not dead.'"

He lived, thanks to the skill of his doctors, but also because of his positive attitude. His example proved to me that every day we have the choice to live fully. Attitude is everything.

✝ A Very Good Dog Tale ✝

Mary and her husband Jim had a dog, Lucky, who was quite a character. Whenever they had company for a weekend, they would warn their friends not to leave luggage open because Lucky would help himself to whatever struck his fancy. Inevitably, someone would forget and something would end up missing.

They would go to Lucky's toy box in the basement and there would be the treasure, amid Lucky's favorites. Lucky stashed his finds in his toy box and was very particular that they remain in the box.

When Mary learned she had breast cancer, something told her she was going to die of this disease. She was sure it was fatal.

She scheduled the double mastectomy, fear shadowing her. The night before she was to enter the hospital, she cuddled with Lucky. A thought struck her: What would happen to Lucky?

Although the three-year-old dog liked Jim, he was Mary's dog through and through. If I die, Lucky will be abandoned, Mary thought. He won't understand that I didn't want to leave him. The notion made her sadder than thinking of her death.

The double mastectomy was harder on Mary than her doctors had anticipated; she was hospitalized for over two weeks. Jim took Lucky for evening walks faithfully but the dog merely drooped, whining and miserable. Finally, the day came for Mary to leave the hospital.

She arrived home so exhausted she could not even make it up the steps to her bedroom. Jim made his wife comfortable on the couch and left her to nap. Lucky stood watch over Mary but he did not come to her when she called. It made Mary sad but sleep overcame her.

When Mary woke, she could not move her head and her body felt heavy and hot. She could not understand what was wrong. Panic soon gave way to laughter when Mary realized the problem.

She was covered, literally blanketed, with every treasure Lucky owned. While she slept, the sorrowing dog made trip after trip to the basement bringing his beloved mistress his favorite things in life. He had swathed her with his love.

Mary forgot about dying. Instead, she and Lucky began living again, walking further and further together every night.

It has been twelve years and Mary is cancer-free. Lucky? He still steals treasures and stashes them in his toy box but Mary remains his greatest treasure.

♱ The Old Phone ♱

When I was quite young, my father had one of the first telephones in our neighborhood. I remember the polished, old case fastened to the wall. The shiny receiver hung on the side of the box. I was too little to reach the telephone, but used to listen with fascination when my mother talked to it.

Then I discovered that somewhere inside the wonderful device lived an amazing person. Her name was "Information Please" and there was nothing she did not know. Information Please could supply anyone's number and the correct time.

My personal experience with the genie-in-a-bottle came one day while my mother was visiting a neighbor. Amusing myself at the tool bench in the basement, I whacked my finger with a hammer. The pain was terrible, but there seemed no point in crying because there was no one home to give sympathy.

I moped through the house sucking my throbbing finger, finally arriving at the stairway. The telephone appeared. I dragged the footstool from the parlor to the landing, climbed up, unhooked the receiver, and pressed it to my ear.

"Information Please," I tiptoed to talk up to the mouthpiece situated above my head.

A click and a small clear voice spoke into my ear, "Information."

"I hurt my finger," I wailed into the phone; the tears came readily enough since I had an audience.

"Isn't your mother home?" queried the voice.

"Nobody's home but me," I blubbered.

"Are you bleeding?" the voice inquired.

"No," I replied. "I hit my finger with the hammer and it hurts."

"Can you open the icebox?" she asked.

I said I could.

"Then chip off a bit of ice and hold it to your finger," the voice instructed.

After that, I called Information Please for everything. I asked for help with my geography. She helped me with my math. She told me the pet chipmunk I had caught in the park would eat fruit and nuts.

Then, there was the time our pet canary died. I called Information Please and related the sad story. She listened patiently and then said things grown-ups say to soothe a child. I was not consoled and asked, "Why is it that birds should sing so beautifully and bring joy to a family, only to end up as a heap of feathers on the bottom of a cage?"

She must have sensed my deep concern for she offered quietly, "Wayne, there are other worlds to sing in." Somehow I felt better.

Another day I was on the telephone, "Information Please?"

"Information," the familiar tone answered.

"How do I spell 'fix'?" I asked and she came through as usual.

This occurred in a small town in the Northwest. When I turned nine, we moved cross-country and I missed my friend. Information Please lived in the old wooden box back home and I never thought of trying the shiny new phone sitting on the hall table.

As I entered my teens, memories of those childhood conversations never left me. In moments of doubt and perplexity, I recalled the serene sense of security I had then. I appreciated how patient and kind she was to have spent her time on a little boy.

A few years later, on my way west to college, my plane put down in Seattle. I had about a half-hour between planes. I spent fifteen minutes on the phone with my sister who lived there. Afterwards, without thinking, I dialed my hometown operator and said, "Information Please."

Miraculously, I recognized the small, clear voice, "Information."

I had not planned this, but I heard myself ask, "Could you, please, tell me how to spell 'fix'?"

After a long pause, a soft-spoken answer, "I guess your finger must have healed by now."

I laughed. "So, it's really you," I said. "I wonder if you have any idea how much you meant to me during that time?"

"I wonder if you know how much your call meant to me? I never had children and I used to look forward to your calls," she replied.

I told her how often I thought of her over the years and asked if I could call her again when I returned to visit my sister.

"Please do. Ask for Sally."

Three months later, I was in Seattle. A different voice answered, "Information." I asked for Sally and stated my name.

"Are you a friend?" she inquired.

"Yes, a very old friend," I answered.

"I'm sorry to have to tell you. Sally had been working part-time the last few years because she was sick. She died five weeks ago."

Before I could hang up, she said, "Wait a minute, did you say your name was Wayne?"

"Yes," I responded absently.

"Sally left a message for you. She wrote it down in case you called. Let me read it to you, 'Tell him there are other worlds to sing in. He'll know what I mean.'"

I thanked her and hung up. I knew what Sally meant: Distance did not separate us anymore and I did not need the telephone line to hear her sing.

Never underestimate the impression you may make on others.

Whose life have you touched today?

♱ A Pastor's Message to His Congregation ♱

Have confidence that I will endeavor to do all to the glory of God and the congregation.

Pray that I may not yield to pride or fear. Be mindful that Christian ministers are a special target for the devil, for through the fall of one he can achieve the fall of many.

Ask God to endow me with the Holy Spirit that I may speak His Law fearlessly and proclaim His Gospel enthusiastically.

Should you or one of your dear ones be sick, tell me about it. Do not expect me to learn of your needs through dreams or revelations.

Should something in my life appear to be dishonorable or out of harmony with my profession, tell me about it in a faithful spirit. You will find me responsive to every sincere word of helpful admonition.

Do not expect me to be a perfect person, as I am far from it. Should you wish to speak about my imperfections, I earnestly petition that you speak to the Lord about them.

Do not expect me to say to you only that for which your ears itch, but that which your heart needs.

Do not judge my motives or think evil of me as the basis of hearsay. Come to me and get the facts. If I am in error, I will be the first to strive for improvements.

Do not tattle on others. If others have offended you or done evil, go to them and tell them. Keep in mind, however, that "wherein you judge another, you condemn thyself." Whatever you say to another, say it only to be helpful.

While I shall always endeavor to be of one spirit with you, I cannot always share your views on every issue, so give me the right to mine.

Do not accuse me of favoritism, as I am resolved to treat everyone alike, without respect of person.

Do not expect to hear only good things about me. "The disciple is not above the master, nor the servant above the Lord." They said a lot of things about the Lord that were not nice.

Give me the benefit of your friendship. Though I do not expect all to be fond of me, I expect you to love me for the sake of my work. Try to remember that the pastor has no pastor, and that he loves to have the warm friendship of those he serves.

Keep in mind that Satan celebrates when a spiteful and unspiritual relationship exists between pastor and people. Therefore, I ask you to realize that by preserving my honor you preserve God's honor.

♰ Tears: The Measure of a Woman's Strength ♰

A little boy asked his mother, "Why are you crying?"

"Because I'm a woman," she told him.

"I don't understand," he said.

His Mom hugged him and said, "And you never will."

Later, the little boy asked his father, "Why does mother seem to cry for no reason?"

"Women cry for no reason," his dad replied flatly.

The little boy grew up and became a man, still wondering why women cry. Finally he put in a call to God. When God answered, he asked, "God, why do women cry so easily?"

God said:

"When I made woman, she had to be special. I made her shoulders strong enough to carry the weight of the world, yet gentle enough to give comfort.

"I gave her an inner strength to endure childbirth and the rejection that many times comes from her children.

"I gave her a toughness that allows her to keep going even when everyone else gives up, and take care of her family through sickness and fatigue without complaining.

"I gave her the sensitivity to love her children under any circumstances, even when her child has hurt her badly.

"I gave her strength to carry her husband through his faults and fashioned her from his rib to protect his heart.

"I gave her wisdom to know that a good husband never hurts his wife, but sometimes tests her strengths and her resolve to stand beside him unfalteringly.

"And, finally, I gave her a tear to shed. This is hers exclusively to use whenever it is needed.

"You see, my son, the beauty of a woman is not in the clothes she wears, the figure she carries, or the way she combs her hair. The beauty of a woman must be seen in her eyes, because that is the doorway to her heart, the place where love resides."

✢ The Pickle Jar ✢

The pickle jar, as far back as I can remember, sat on the floor beside the dresser in my parents' bedroom. When preparing for bed, Dad would empty his pockets and toss his coins into the jar.

As a small boy, I was fascinated at the sounds the coins made as they were dropped into the jar. They landed with a merry jingle when the jar was almost empty. Then the tones gradually muted to a dull thud as the jar was filled.

I used to squat on the floor in front of the jar and admire the copper and silver circles that glinted like a pirate's treasure when the sun poured through the bedroom window. When the jar was filled, Dad would sit at the kitchen table and roll the coins before taking them to the bank.

Taking them to the bank was always a big production. Stacked neatly in a small cardboard box, the coins were placed between Dad and me on the seat of his old truck.

Each and every time, as we drove to the bank, Dad would look at me hopefully. "Those coins are going to keep you out of the textile mill, son. You're going to do better than me. This old mill town's not going to hold you back."

Also, each and every time, as he slid the box of rolled coins across the bank counter to the cashier, he would grin proudly. "These are for my son's college fund. He'll not work at the mill his entire life like me."

We would celebrate each deposit by stopping for an ice cream. I got chocolate and Dad vanilla. When the clerk at the ice cream parlor handed

Dad his change, he would show me the few coins nestled in his palm. "When we get home, we'll start filling the jar again."

He always let me drop the first coins into the empty jar. As they rattled around with a brief, happy jingle, we grinned at each other. "You'll get to college on pennies, nickels, dimes, and quarters," he said. "But you'll get there. I'll see to that."

The years passed. I finished college and took a job in another town. Once, while visiting my parents, I used the phone in their bedroom; and noticed that the pickle jar was gone. It had served its purpose and had been removed.

A lump rose in my throat as I stared at the spot beside the dresser where the jar had always stood. My dad was a man of few words, and never lectured me on the values of determination, perseverance, and faith.

The pickle jar had taught me these virtues far more eloquently than the most flowery words could have done. When I married, I told my wife Susan about the significance the lowly pickle jar had played in my life as a boy. In my mind, it defined, more than anything else, how much my dad had loved me.

No matter how rough things got, Dad continued to doggedly drop his coins into the jar. Even the summer when Dad got laid off from the mill, and Mama had to serve dried beans several times a week, not a single dime was taken from the jar.

To the contrary, as Dad looked across the table at me, pouring catsup over my beans to make them more palatable, he became more determined than ever to make a way out for me. "When you finish college, son," he told me, his eyes glistening, "You'll never have to eat beans again unless you want to."

The first CHRISTmas after our daughter Jessica was born, we spent the holiday with my parents. After dinner, Mom and Dad sat next to each other on the sofa, taking turns cuddling their first grandchild.

Jessica began to whimper softly, and Susan took her from Dad's arms. "She probably needs to be changed," she said, carrying the baby into my parents' bedroom to diaper her. When Susan came back into the living room, there was a strange mist in her eyes.

She handed Jessica to Dad before taking my hand and leading me into the room. "Look," she said softly, her eyes directing me to a spot on the floor beside the dresser. To my amazement, there, as if it had never been removed, stood the old pickle jar, the bottom already covered with coins.

I walked over to the pickle jar, dug down into my pocket, and pulled out a fistful of coins. With a gamut of emotions choking me, I dropped the coins into the jar. I looked up and saw that Dad, carrying Jessica, had slipped quietly into the room. Our eyes locked, and I knew he was feeling the same emotions I felt. Neither of us could speak.

✟ The Yellow Shirt ✟

The baggy yellow shirt had long sleeves, four extra-large pockets trimmed in black thread, and snaps up the front. It was faded from years of wear, but still in decent shape. I found it in 1963 when I was home from college on CHRISTmas break rummaging through bags of clothes Mom intended to give away.

"You're not taking that old thing are you?" Mom said when she saw me packing the yellow shirt. "I wore that when I was pregnant with your brother in 1954."

"It's exactly the thing to wear over my clothes during art class, Mom. Thanks." I slipped it into my suitcase before she could object.

The yellow shirt became part of my college wardrobe. I loved it. After graduation, I wore the yellow shirt the day I moved into my new apartment and on Saturday mornings when I cleaned.

The next year, I married. When I became pregnant, I wore the yellow shirt during big belly days. I missed Mom and the rest of my family, since we were in Colorado and they were in Illinois. But that shirt helped. I smiled, remembering that Mother had worn it when she was pregnant, fifteen years earlier.

That CHRISTmas, mindful of the warm feelings the shirt had given me, I patched one elbow, wrapped it in holiday paper, and sent it to Mom. When Mom wrote to thank me for her "real" gifts, she said the yellow shirt was lovely. She never mentioned it again.

The next year, my husband, daughter, and I stopped at Mom and Dad's to pick up some furniture. Days later, when we uncrated the kitchen table, I noticed something yellow taped to its bottom: the shirt.

And so the pattern was set.

On our next visit home, I secretly placed the shirt under Mom and Dad's mattress. I do not know how long it took for her to find it, but almost two years passed before I discovered it under the base of our living room floor lamp. The yellow shirt was precisely what I needed while refinishing furniture. The walnut stains added character.

In 1975, my husband and I divorced. With three children, I prepared to move back to Illinois. As I packed, a deep depression overtook me. I wondered if I could make it on my own, if I would find a job.

I paged through the Bible, looking for comfort. In Ephesians, I read, "Use every piece of God's armor to resist the enemy whenever he attacks, and when it is over, you will be standing up."

I tried to picture myself wearing God's armor, but what I saw was the stained yellow shirt. Slowly, it dawned on me. Was not my mother's love a piece of God's armor? My courage was renewed.

Unpacking in our new home, I knew I had to return the shirt to her. The next time I visited, I tucked it in her bottom dresser drawer.

Meanwhile, I found a good job at a radio station. A year later, I discovered the yellow shirt hidden in a rag bag in my cleaning closet. Something new had been added. Embroidered in bright green across the breast pocket were the words, "I belong to Pat."

Not to be outdone, I got out my embroidery materials and added an apostrophe and seven letters. The shirt proudly proclaimed, "I belong to Pat's Mother."

I did not stop there. I zigzagged the frayed seams and had a friend mail the updated shirt in a fancy box to Mom from Arlington, Virginia. We enclosed an official-looking letter from "The Institute for the Destitute" announcing that she was the recipient of an award for good deeds. I would have given anything to see Mom's face when she opened the box. But, of course, she never mentioned it.

Two years later, I remarried. The day of our wedding, Harold and I put our car in a friend's garage to avoid practical jokers. After the wedding, while my husband drove to our honeymoon suite, I reached for a pillow to rest my head. It felt lumpy. I unzipped the case and found, wrapped in wedding paper, the yellow shirt. Inside a pocket was a note: "Read John 14:27-29. I love you both, Mother."

That night I paged through the Bible and found the verses: "I am leaving you with a gift: peace of mind and heart. And the peace I give isn't fragile like the peace the world gives. So don't be troubled or afraid. Remember what I told you: I am going away, but I will come back to you again. If you really love me, you will be very happy for me, for now I can go to the Father, who is greater than I am. I have told you these things before they happen so that when they do, you will believe in me."

The shirt was Mother's final gift. She had known for three months that she had terminal Lou Gehrig's disease. She died the following year at age fifty-seven.

I was tempted to send the yellow shirt with her to her grave. But I am glad I did not, because it is a vivid reminder of the love-filled game she and I played for sixteen years. Besides, my older daughter is in college majoring in art. And every art student needs a baggy yellow shirt with big pockets.

God Brews the Coffee, Not the Cups

A group of alumni, highly established in their careers, gathered to visit their old professor. Conversation soon turned into complaints about the stresses of life.

The professor went to the kitchen and returned with a large pot of coffee and an assortment of cups: glass, porcelain, plastic, crystal, some plain, some expensive, and others quite exquisite. Offering the coffee, he asked them to help themselves.

When his former students had a cup of coffee in hand, he said: "If you noticed, the nice looking, expensive cups were taken, leaving behind the plain and cheap ones. While it is normal for you to want only the best for yourselves, that is the source of your stress.

"Be assured that the cup itself adds no quality to the coffee in most cases; it is simply more expensive and, in some cases, even hides what we drink. What you really wanted was coffee, not the cup, but you consciously chose the best cups and then began eyeing each other's cups.

"Consider this: Life is the coffee and your jobs, money, and status are the cups. They are merely tools to hold and contain life, and the type of cup we have does not define, nor change, the quality of life we live.

"Sometimes, by concentrating only on the cup, we fail to enjoy the coffee God has provided us."

Enjoy your coffee.

♱ The Mask: A Journal Entry ♱

By Walter A. Glover, MTS, Chaplain
St. Vincent Jennings Hospital, North Vernon, Indiana

What comes to mind?

Who visits your mirror?

Imagine: Clowns at a summer big-top circus. Painted-on faces frolic with balloons and funny antics. Who is inside the clown's head, behind the face? Are secrets veiled with a veneer of grease?

Calendars turn: Halloween howls as youthful ghouls knock. Are you scared by the masks? Or, do you see gaiety of kids in pretend? Who is behind their mask? Have the child's parents just divorced? Was there a recent grand-parent death? Squeals of laughter; sometimes shrieks of fear. For sure, we hear boldness around treats lest the unwary greeter be tricked. What's going on inside the homeowner's head? Did he or she lose their job that day? Was a friend diagnosed with cancer?

Snow falls: Santa takes his throne. The promise of presents after inquiry around goodness and badness almost rings like reconciliation liturgy. A spoken, "Ho, ho, ho," wells from a whiskered reddened face concealed by bushy eyebrows and a stocking red cap. Is Santa jolly? Does he carry an unspoken burden? Has his own child died? Was he abused as a teen by a teacher?

Who is in my mirror? Who is in yours? A mask, or simply an unshaven un-made up face blessed by a countenance of peace and joy?

In a period musical, the Parisian anti-hero dies violently after freeing himself from a mask.

Holy Thursday: "A young man," presumably the evangelist Mark, in his gospel chapter fourteen, fled from Jesus' arrest scene. He was disrobed as he ran, scripture informs us. No clothing. No mask. No friends to companion him. Alone, he fled into the dark of the margin. His friend, his Savior, was about to die. Desertion time for a disciple.

If desertion time awaits, do I mask up or tread naked? Do masks deny reality? Do masks confuse others? Do they deceive those who put them on?

We are naked before the mirror . . . before each other . . . before God. Masks, the opera phantom confessed, are for a season. Revelation eclipses mystery. Mark would learn this, as do we.

Do I know who you are? Do you?
Do I know who I am? Do you?
Do we know who each other are?

Do masks, ghosts, secrets hold us back?

The Author of Life, of Truth, of Beauty, He knows us inside-out. Mask-less, we stand before Him.

♰ Can You Sleep When the Wind Blows? ♰

A farmer, owning land along the seacoast, constantly advertised for hired hands. Most people were reluctant to work on farms along the coast. They dreaded the awful storms that raged across the ocean, wreaking havoc on the buildings and crops.

As the farmer interviewed applicants for the job, he received a steady stream of refusals. Finally, a short, thin man, well past middle age, approached. "Are you a good farm hand?" the farmer asked.

"Well, I can sleep when the wind blows," answered the little man.

Although puzzled by this answer, the farmer, desperate for help, hired him. The little man worked well around the farm, busy from dawn to dusk, and the farmer felt satisfied with the man's work.

One night the wind howled loudly in from offshore. Jumping out of bed, the farmer grabbed a lantern and rushed next door to the hired hand's sleeping quarters. He shook the little man and yelled, "Get up, a storm is coming. Tie things down before they blow away."

The little man rolled over in bed and said firmly, "No, sir. I told you, I can sleep when the wind blows." Enraged by the response, the farmer was tempted to fire him on the spot. Instead, he hurried outside to prepare for the storm.

To his amazement, he discovered that the haystacks had been covered with tarpaulins. The cows were in the barn, the chickens in the coops, the doors barred, and the shutters tightly secured. Everything was tied down so nothing could blow away. The farmer then understood what his hired hand meant, so he returned to his bed to also sleep while the wind blew.

We secure ourselves against the storms of life by grounding ourselves in the Word of God.

✟ Whose Hands Is It In? ✟

A basketball in my hands is worth about $19.
A basketball in Michael Jordan's hands is worth about $33 million.
It depends on whose hands it's in.

A baseball in my hands is worth about $6.
A baseball in Mark McGwire's hands is worth $19 million.
It depends on whose hands it's in.

A tennis racket is useless in my hands.
A tennis racket in Serena Williams's hands is worth a championship.
It depends on whose hands it's in.

A rod in my hands will keep away a wild animal.
A rod in Moses's hands will part the mighty sea.
It depends on whose hands it's in.

A slingshot in my hands is a kid's toy.
A slingshot in David's hand is a mighty weapon.
It depends on whose hands it's in.

Two fish and five loaves of bread in my hands is a couple of fish sandwiches.
Two fish and five loaves of bread in God's hands will feed thousands.
It depends on whose hands it's in.

Nails in my hands might produce a birdhouse.
Nails in Jesus Christ's hands will produce salvation for the entire world.
It depends on whose hands it's in.

As you see, it depends on whose hands it's in.
Place your worries, fears, hopes, dreams, families, and relationships in God's hands because . . . it depends on whose hands it's in.

This message is now in your hands. What will you do with it?
It depends on whose hands it's in!

About the Author

The author resides in Charlottesville, Virginia with his lovely wife, Malgosia, an architect specializing in designing intelligent homes. Their daughter Marta, a psychologist, lives in Chicago with her husband, Brian, a National Science Foundation scholar at Northwestern University. Ralph credits his son-in-law, Brian, with conception of the "e-Soup" title for the book series.

Spiritual e-Soup Ministry

e-Lectronic e-Vangelism
Spreading the Good News via the Internet

You can involve yourself in the ministry:

Subscribe to Today's Inspirational Message
Volunteer as a Prayer Partner
Present Prayer Requests for family and friends
Enroll in our campaign to "Put Christ back into CHRISTmas"
Schedule Ralph for speaking or book-signing engagements
Submit a message for inclusion in volume II of *Spiritual e-Soup*

You can purchase books autographed by author Ralph Barnett:

Spiritual e-Soup: A Compilation of Inspirational Messages from the Internet

Spiritual Humor e-Soup: A Compilation of Amusing Messages from the Internet

Humorous e-Soup: A Compilation of Jokes from the Internet

Pre-publication CHRISTmas gift certificates for books

Books on CD including original e-mail graphics

Pre-publication promotional offers

You can purchase:

Spiritual e-Soup Ministry logo merchandise
"Put Christ back into CHRISTmas" logo merchandise
Spiritual First Aid Kits
CHRISTmas Oplatek

You can raise funds for your group or organization:

Book signings and speaking engagements
Book sales
Put Christ back into CHRISTmas logo merchandise
Spiritual First Aid Kits
Spiritual e-Soup Ministry logo merchandise
CHRISTmas Oplatek
Autographed book donations for door prizes, raffles, or auctions

For more information:

e-mail: ralphbarnett@e-soupministry.com

website: www.e-soupministry.com (under construction)

Order Form

E-mail orders
info@e-soupministry.com

Website orders
www.e-soupministry.com

Telephone orders
847 606-0854

Postal orders
e-Soup Publishing
Order Fulfillment Department
994 Glenwood Station Lane
Charlottesville, VA 22901

Note: Books will be autographed by Ralph Barnett

Send _______ copy/s of *Spiritual e-Soup* @ $14.95 = $ ___________
Send _______ copy/s of *Spiritual e-Soup* CD @ 5.95 = ___________
Send _______ copy/s of *Spiritual Humor e-Soup* @ 14.95 = ___________
Send _______ copy/s of *Spiritual Humor* CD @ 5.95 = ___________
Send _______ copy/s of *Humorous e-Soup* @ 14.95 = ___________
Send _______ copy/s of *Humorous e-Soup* CD @ 5.95 = ___________

Total for books and CDs $ ___________

Sales tax in Virginia (multiply total by 5%) $ ___________

Shipping & Handling
United States – $2.00 per book $ ___________
$1.00 per CD $ ___________
International - $5.00 per book $ ___________
$2.50 per CD $ ___________

TOTAL DUE $ ___________

I understand that I may return the products for a full refund for any reason, no questions asked.

Name: ___________________________________

Street: ___________________________________

City, State, Zip: ___________________________________

E-mail: ___________________________________

Phone: (DAY) _________________ (EVE) _________________